Authority Work

AUTHORITY WORK

The Creation, Use, Maintenance, and Evaluation of Authority Records and Files

Robert H. Burger
University Library, Slavic & East European Department
University of Illinois at Urbana-Champaign

Libraries Unlimited, Inc.
Littleton, Colorado
1985

LIBRARIES UNLIMITED, INC.
P.O. Box 263
Littleton, Colorado 80160-0263

Library of Congress Cataloging in Publication Data

Burger, Robert H. (Robert Harold), 1947-
  Authority work.

  Bibliography: p. 115
  Includes index.
  1. Authority files (Cataloging) 2. Library records.
I. Title.
Z693.B87 1985   025.3'22   85-6791
ISBN 0-87287-491-5

Libraries Unlimited books are bound with Type II nonwoven material that meets
and exceeds National Association of State Textbook Administrators' Type II
nonwoven material specifications Class A through E.

To my parents
Vera and Harry Burger

*"For all that has been—thanks;
for all that shall be—yes!"*

—Dag Hammarskjöld

TABLE OF CONTENTS

LIST OF TABLES
AND FIGURES

Tables

Figures

ACKNOWLEDGMENTS

This book owes its existence to many people, some of whom may rue the day that they knowingly or unknowingly gave aid. I am particularly grateful to Lester Asheim, J. L. Divilbiss, Kathryn L. Henderson, F. W. Lancaster, and Linda C. Smith for what I have learned from them in the classroom and outside; to Harry Leich, Larry Miller, and Dmytro Shtohryn, my practical teachers in cataloging; Larry Auld, Michael Gorman, Richard Smiraglia, and Arnold Wajenberg for their patient and thorough reading of earlier drafts of the manuscript and their many helpful comments; to Marianna Tax Choldin for creating a supportive environment in which to work; to the University of Illinois Library Research and Publication Committee for monetary support for manuscript preparation; to Ann Della Porta, Judy Fenly, and Suzanne Liggett of the Library of Congress for initiating me into the challenging world of NACO and LC authority work; to Ruth R. Hansel, for a warm and comfortable place to write and relax; to Patty Hodgins, for a masterful job of copyediting; to Sarah, Margaret, and Nell, my daughters, any one of whom would make fatherhood ideal; to my wife, Ann, who in her sometimes comforting, sometimes spirited way, continues to be my mainstay; and finally to my parents, Vera and Harry Burger, who, although they still don't have a clear notion of what I do, have done more than they realize to give my life meaning and enjoyment.

FOREWORD

I write the foreword to this book by my colleague and friend, Robert Burger, with great pleasure and enthusiasm. These feelings are generated by the regard I have for his work, the timeliness and importance of the subject, and the skill with which he has carried out his task.

Francis Bacon spoke of "virtue ... in authority settled and calm." It is odd that, even now, we should have to argue the importance of authority control and plead for its "virtue." One would have thought that that argument should have been settled well over a century ago, in the course of the disputation between Crestadoro and Panizzi (ah, those fine old English names!) during the Parliamentary hearings on the British Museum Library. It will be recalled that Crestadoro said, in essence, that any fool could do cataloging and, presumably to prove his point, produced numerous examples of his own cataloging. Panizzi then demonstrated that most of the entries had errors and that Crestadoro had in fact shown the necessity for trained catalogers. The point of this musty anecdote for us is that almost all of Crestadoro's errors were in the area of what we would nowadays call authority control. One can make routine and, sometimes, mechanical certain parts of the descriptive cataloging process. What cannot be treated in that manner is the process of assigning works to classes identified by names and titles signifying important collocative instruments which, though practical in their purpose and use, are abstract and theoretically based. It is this razor's edge of the cataloging process which Mr. Burger delineates so skillfully in his book. It is also necessary to see the topic of this book as a useful corrective to the bosh which is still sometimes written about automated systems and their fancied ability to dispense with the disciplines of conventional cataloging. One of the weariest cliches of automation is the slogan, "garbage in, garbage out." Though dreary, it is also true. The fact is that the manipulation of random nonstandard bibliographic data will yield, at best, erratic results. At its frequent worst it will fail to connect related data and will hide needed materials from the would-be reader. Traditional cataloging practice contained much that was redundant and much that was obsolete. Authority control does not happen to fall into either of these categories and, here as in the rest of life, care should be taken to distinguish between babies and bathwater.

An interesting feature of this book is that it is not only descriptive but also projective. Mr. Burger looks forward to uses of authority control which are, at present, little more than gleams in his eye. He discusses alluring and plausible lines of development such as the possible applications in measurement and evaluation.

We see authority control, through his eyes, as more than a modern rereading of established practice. It becomes an important feature of up-to-date and, as yet, nonexistent bibliographic control.

In the fifth chapter of this book, Mr. Burger examines a number of current on-line authority systems. This survey and analysis is not only of descriptive interest but also reveals the immense difficulties in making comparisons where the systems being compared are inadequately documented and rapidly changing. It is here that we see most clearly that Mr. Burger's topic is as up-to-date as can be. The difficulties in comparison are typical of a changing, developing, and new field. The author combines his knowledge of the past and his present practical experience to show where we are and where we are going in this challenging and absorbing area of librarianship.

Berowne (in *Love's Labour's Lost*) thinks that "authority from other's books" is the only reward of "continual plodders." In this far from plodding book, Mr. Burger shows us that such authority is the key to bibliographic control and, hence, to the access to knowledge which is the basis of all good librarianship.

Michael Gorman
Professor of Library Administration &
Director of General Services
University Library
University of Illinois at Urbana-Champaign

INTRODUCTION

In spite of its detractors,[1] authority control has come to be recognized as an essential component of any on-line catalog.[2] With the acknowledgement of the necessity of authority control has come an increasing interest in the activity surrounding this process. The increase in the number of articles on authority control,[3] the special conferences dealing with this subject, development of MARC formats for the exchange of authority information on magnetic tape, and increased interest at the national level in essential components of a national network,[4] all eloquently and forcefully attest to the centrality of authority control in the catalog's future.

My approach to the discussion of authority control and authority work is process oriented—I examine the processes used to create, maintain, use, and evaluate authority records. Although not codified, these processes taken together have come to be called authority work.[5] Authority work consists of determining the form of access points and recording information about such decisions. Authority control is achieved when headings in a catalog are consistent and when a mechanism (the authority file) and related cataloging policies have been established to ensure this consistency. I also see a need to describe existing machine-readable authority systems in order to focus on the state of the art and draw comparisons among some existing systems.

I devote a lengthy Appendix at the end of this book to the MARC authority format. Some may argue that this is unnecessary, since such information is already available either in the document published by the Library of Congress[6] or in documents issued by the major bibliographic networks—OCLC, the Research Libraries Information Network (RLIN), and the Washington Library Network (WLN). But after presenting workshops on the MARC authority format for four years under the auspices of ILLINET, the Illinois state reference network, I have become convinced of the need for an explanation different from that given in the above-mentioned documents. Further, in the Appendix I attempt to single out specific parts of the format as more important than others. This is a personal choice, not one sanctioned by the Library of Congress or any other body. This concentration on the various parts has evolved from experience in writing specifications for programmers who will use the format for an on-line catalog at the University of Illinois at Urbana-Champaign. Others with experience in other systems may emphasize other parts.

Finally, in this volume I try to offer some structure to the futuristic discussions about authority control and what it means for catalogs and libraries. We need to see where we are in authority control, where the weak parts are, what parts need strengthening and more research, where we have to apply more effort, and where we need more experience. This book does not seek primarily to break new ground, but rather to ground us more solidly in the body of knowledge we now possess.

NOTES

1. Mitch Freeman, "A Conversation with Frederick G. Kilgour," *Technicalities* 1(7):5 (June 1981).

2. Mary W. Ghikas, ed., *Authority Control: The Key to Tomorrow's Catalog; Proceedings of the 1979 Library and Information Technology Association Institutes* (Phoenix, Ariz.: Oryx Press, 1982).

3. As a rough measure of this trend I examined the number of articles on authority control that appeared in *Library Literature* between 1977 and 1984. See also Larry Auld, "Authority Control: An Eighty Year Review," *Library Resources and Technical Services* 26:319-330 (October/December 1982).

4. Council on Library Resources, Inc., Bibliographic Service Development Program, "An Integrated Consistent Authority File Service for Nationwide Use," *Library of Congress Information Bulletin* 39:244-248 (July 11, 1980); Wayne E. Davison, "The WLN/RLG/LC Linked Systems Project," *Information Technology and Libraries* 2:34-46 (March 1983).

5. "An Integrated Consistent Authority File Service," p. 248. Authority work has also been given a narrower meaning by Helen F. Schmierer. In "The Relationship of Authority Control to the Library Catalog," *Illinois Libraries* 62:599-603 (September 1980) she states: "No matter how one defines or identifies library cataloging activities, ... the two activities of determining the form of access points and recording information about such decisions are somehow or somewhere included. These two activities are here referred to collectively as 'authority work.' "

6. *Authorities: A MARC Format,* 1st ed. (Washington, D.C.: Library of Congress, Processing Services, 1981).

1

AUTHORITY CONTROL: GENERAL PRINCIPLES

DEFINITION OF AUTHORITY WORK

The term *authority work* is used to refer to several processes related to the cataloging of library materials. As far as can be determined, no comprehensive definition of the scope and purpose of the various processes designated by the term has yet been stated.[1] However, from the various uses of *authority work* in the literature we may infer that it consists of at least five complex processes:

1. the creation of *authority records* (which are used in turn to create authoritative bibliographic records)

2. the gathering of records into an *authority file*

3. the linking of that file to a bibliographic file; together these form an *authority system*

4. the maintenance of the authority file and system

5. the evaluation of the file and system

Together these processes constitute the central part of the cataloging system and are the major aspect of the activity that is crucial to the retrieval of items from a catalog. Authority work enables authority control to occur. Let us examine the separate processes briefly; they will be expanded upon in the following chapters.

AUTHORITY CONTROL

Catalog records consist of three parts:

1. access points—for the work

2. bibliographic description—for the item at hand

3. location—for the individual library's holdings

Authority control is directed at the first part, access points, and serves two purposes for the catalog, the finding function and the gathering function. That is, the catalog serves

1. To enable a person to find a book of which either

    (A) the author
    (B) the title   is known
    (C) the subject

2. To show what the library has

    (D) by a given author
    (E) on a given subject
    (F) in a given kind of literature.[2]

This classic formulation by Cutter was rephrased by the authors of the Paris Principles (1961) to read:

2. Functions of the Catalogue

    The catalogue should be an efficient instrument for ascertaining

    2.1 Whether the library contains a particular book specified by

        (a) its author and title, or
        (b) if the author is not named in the book, its title alone, or
        (c) if the author and title are inappropriate or insufficient for identification, a suitable substitute for the title; and

    2.2 (a) which works by a particular author, and which editions of a particular work are in the library.[3]

Helen Schmierer has summarized these two statements to read:

1. the library catalog should enable a user to ascertain if the library has a particular item and

2. the library catalog should show what items the library has that share a common characteristic.[4]

Both of these purposes of the catalog as stated by Schmierer require access points. An access point is a standardized name, personal or corporate; uniform title; standardized subject name; call number; and standardized name of form (internal, e.g., *poetry*, or external, e.g., *dictionary*). The form of these access points must be unique, in order to differentiate them from similar access points, and must also be consistent, so that the "common characteristic" of bibliographic items linked by them appears the same way throughout the catalog. Without both uniqueness and consistency, retrieval from the catalog will not be optimal and in some cases may even be impossible.

In Chapter 2 I will discuss in more detail the kinds of information that constitute an authority record. But let me summarize the role of the authority record by listing specific characteristics.

The authority record

1. records a form of access point that is prescribed by the cataloging code in effect and that is used to permit the uniform application of this form for future additions to the catalog that also use that access point for retrieval

2. ensures the collocation of records in a bibliographic file that have the same access point

3. ensures the issuance of standardized bibliographic surrogates (i.e., a catalog record, as defined above)

4. documents decisions taken with respect to the form of access point, so that the laborious and demanding task of determining the current form of entry is done only once, at the first occurrence of that access point in the catalog

5. can record, as cross-references, variant manifestations of access points caused by natural occurrences (marriages, deaths, etc.), different sets of cataloging rules, and local policy

Some have argued that authority work simply consists of only two of the activities described above: determining the form of access points and recording information about such decisions.[5] For the individual cataloger, authority work may stop at this point. But for the products of the cataloger's labor to be used, several other steps must be taken.

Once an authority record is created, it must be integrated into an existing authority file. The very process of integration may cause alterations in the recently formed access point. At the time of integration, the cataloger may discover that the form of access point chosen is identical to the form of another access point that has already been formulated. In such a case, alteration of the last-chosen form, or both forms, is usually necessary. This ensures that the authority file does not contain ambiguous information, such as two authority records each with identical forms but obviously concerning different entities.

Furthermore, to create an authority system, the authority file itself needs to be linked in some fashion to the bibliographic file. In card, book, or microform catalogs, such links are implicit rather than explicit. What makes the link implicit in printed catalogs is the presence of the identical form of name, title, or series on both the authority card and the catalog card. Some libraries instruct those who prepare authority records to transcribe the call number of the book whose processing initiated the recording of the name on the authority card. In other libraries, the authority record, if it may be called such, is identical with the official catalog. In such catalogs, there is no authority file per se, and the official catalog functions as the authority file.

In machine catalogs this linkage has also been effected in various ways and in various degrees of elegance. Ideally, there is a separate authority file with a machine link between an authority record and the bibliographic records that use that name as an access point. In other machine systems, there is an authority file and a bibliographic file, without a linkage between both files.

An element of authority work discussed too infrequently is maintenance of the authority system once it is in place. Maintenance is often ignored in the planning stages of authority files, partly because maintenance is often done by clerical personnel who have little voice in the planning of authority systems. Also, maintenance is often erroneously thought of as a secondary activity that can somehow be taken care of once the authority file is in place.

Since change is a primary characteristic of authority work, the control and processing of change should also be primary. Changes are constantly occurring. There are changes of names, mistakes to be corrected, new information available on names, and new relationships to be noted and implemented within the system. Such changes affect individual authority records, bibliographic records, and linkages between authority records within the authority file as well as linkages between the authority file and the bibliographic file. With the processing of serials, there occur problems with analytics, variant titles, subseries, and other types of hierarchical and chronological relationships that change and that must be recorded. All this is part of maintenance.

Evaluation of name authorities seems to be an overlooked topic in the literature of authority work. There are hundreds of articles on the evaluation of subject authority systems, especially those that deal with controlled vocabularies, and some of the principles useful in subject authority work are applicable to name authority work as well. But the purposes of name authorities and those of subject authorities differ. Evaluation of the unique aspects of name authority work have yet to be discerned and described in any coherent manner. Chapter 4 deals with this barely perceived problem. Essentially, evaluation is discussed in relation to the preparation of authority records, the description of completed authority records, and the behavior of authority records and files.

Another aspect of evaluation explored in Chapter 4 is the economic evaluation of authority systems. The decision to use the official catalog as the authority system is essentially a cost/benefit decision. It saves the library money because the extra costs of planning for, storing, maintaining, and using a separate authority file are avoided. Benefits may be sacrificed, however, when such a decision is made.

All these five elements, then—creation of authority records, formation of such records into a file, the linking of that file to a bibliographic file to form a system, the maintenance of the file and system, and the constant evaluation of the file and system—constitute authority work. It is curious that authority work is beginning to arouse such interest among librarians and information specialists. Part of the reason undoubtedly is the growing sophistication of our machine systems and catalogs. Part can also be ascribed to the adoption of *Anglo-American Cataloguing Rules,* second edition (AACR2), by the Anglo-American library community. But whatever the reasons for the growing interest in authority work, we must not forget that it does have a history.

AN HISTORICAL PERSPECTIVE: FROM SYNDETIC STRUCTURE OF RECORDS TO SYNDETIC STRUCTURE OF ENTRIES

In general terms we may say that the concept and practice of authority control has moved from a syndetic structure of records in Cutter's day to the present syndetic structure of entries.[6] What does this mean?

The pre-machine technology catalogs existing up to the postwar era primarily took the form of cards or books. Bibliographic records in such catalogs were created individually and connected or linked to other *records* in the catalog. This was done because the only individual element by which to connect bibliographic information was the individual bibliographic record. There was essentially one file, and within this file records, not entries, were linked. The linkage took place by collocation (records filed together) within the catalog or by means of notes on catalog records specifying that the record for which the note was written was linked in some way to another record. The series-added entry, for example, linked individual bibliographic records by filing them all within one sequence under the same entry. In this manner, the records for which a series-added entry was made were linked with other records in the catalog by collocation. Similarly, a work that appeared under different forms of title, such as a translation, was collocated in the file by use of a uniform title. Records indicating that they were translations of other works would be collocated in one place in the catalog by filing under, say, the title of the original.

So in the pre-machine technology catalogs, linkage took place primarily by collocation within the file and was assisted by references (such as the reference card that noted the change in the name of a corporate body) or notes.

In a machine system, linkages of entries, instead of records, can be carried out. This system does not preclude the linkage of records to other records, but such linkage is often accomplished through the linkage of entries common to both records and not among the records themselves. Michael Gorman has written of the organization of records within what he calls the developed machine system.[7] Within such a system, linkages are effected among entries. Figure 1.1 (p. 8) indicates such linkages.

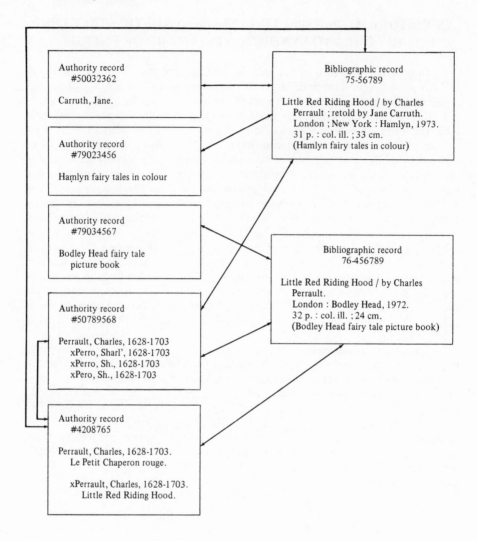

Figure 1.1. Linkages among entries in the developed machine system.

How such a transition has taken place has been described in more detail by Bregzis.[8] Further historical description and analysis of this phenomenon is needed to clarify the development of cataloging theory and the effect of technology on such theory. One way to approach this study is by examining the changes that have occurred in the discussion and treatment of authority control in cataloging textbooks and in cataloging codes over the past century. This examination could then be correlated with the development of and changes in catalog technology. The investigation of this problem is not a central concern of this book, but in order to understand the development of authority control in and of itself, a brief examination is necessary.

Authority Control in Cataloging Codes

For this brief summary, the treatment of authority control can be discussed with reference to two main questions: What is the type of authority control suggested or mandated? and What is the purpose of authority control?

According to the data presented by Auld,[9] the treatment of authority work in cataloging codes has not been a central concern of such documents, nor should it have been. Cutter suggested that "a cataloger's author list, kept alphabetically,"[10] should be established. The purpose of such a list was to avoid "duplication of work. It is a record of the form of name 'in full' which has been adopted, with a note of the authorities consulted and of their variations."[11] The 1908 rules make no mention of authority records but suggest that cross-references should be used.[12] The 1941 *A. L. A. Catalog Rules* provided guidance on the "use and construction of authority cards for headings representing personal and corporate names and uniform titles."[13] The justification for such cards remained "for the convenience of the cataloger."[14] The 1949 rules and *Anglo-American Cataloging Rules,* first edition (AACR1), followed the same pattern of the 1908 rules, "in which cross-references were prescribed but without any suggestion for keeping a record of references used."[15] AACR2 devotes an entire chapter (Chapter 26) to the making of *see from* and *see also from* references*, but without any suggestions as to how these should be used in an authority file. This was, of course, a deliberate omission. All practical aspects (form of catalog, filing, authority procedures, etc.) were consciously left out of AACR2.

The concept of an authority list was first formally discussed by Cutter.[16] More explicit instructions for the construction and maintenance of such a list were given several years later by Fellows.[17] In her text, several pages are devoted to the construction of authority files. The records for such files should consist of slips made for the first book by an author cataloged by a library. Its purpose was "a record of the forms adopted for use in the public catalog."[18] Identical forms were to be used on catalog cards. In general the library should rely on the Library of Congress for the authoritative form of name, except for books cataloged by

---

*These are usually called *see* and *see also* references, respectively. *Authorities: A MARC Format,* however, refers to them as *see from* and *see also from* references. For the sake of consistency, the latter designation will be used throughout the book, except in quoted examples from the Library of Congress of actual authority records.

an individual library for which LC cards were not available.[19] Fellows gives further instructions for the components of such an authority record, such as the form of name, the reference works consulted, and an indication of whether the form of name was found in such consulted works. Reference tracings, history notes for corporate bodies, and the name of the cataloger preparing such slips were also prescribed. In the event that corrections and additions were necessary, they should be carried out clearly, and preferably in red ink! A footnote to this section in Fellows's book states that the entire set of instructions was based on the lectures of Miss Mary E. Hyde of the New York State Library School.

Auld, in his review article,[20] briefly records the types and purposes of other cataloging manuals, including Akers, Mann, Tauber, Osborn, Wynar, Piercy, and Forster. It is interesting that while the briefest mention of authority work is made in codes of cataloging rules, where one does not expect discussion of problems of processing, there is also little extensive discussion of authority work in cataloging manuals. This belies the interest and labor spent on authorities over the past century. The history of the development of authority work in libraries needs to be investigated more thoroughly.

CONCLUSION

The preceding pages have described authority work in libraries. Authority work consists of the creation of authority records, the formation of such records into an authority file, the linking of that file to the bibliographic file to form a system, the maintenance of the authority file and system, and the evaluation of the file and system. The following chapters examine these processes in more detail. But some generalities are in order. Experienced catalogers are painfully aware that cataloging is ceaselessly changing. Codes change, local procedures change, LC rule interpretations change. The products of cataloging are forced to change because of these changes. Authority work is the process whereby librarians attempt to prevent these ceaselessly changing inputs and outputs of the cataloging process from creating bibliographic havoc. Decisions must constantly be made on a micro level with regard to the form that each individual name will take in the file. On the other hand, the cataloger is aware that such decisions are not carved in stone and may—in fact, should—be changed when conditions mandate it. This awareness has led librarians to develop more sophisticated and more streamlined processes by which authority control can be carried out. The results of these efforts are the subject of the following chapters.

NOTES

1.   Authority control is defined simply as "the functions necessary to establish, maintain, and use authority files" on page 245 of Council on Library Resources, Inc., Bibliographic Service Development Program "An Integrated Consistent Authority File Service for Nationwide Use," *Library of Congress Information Bulletin* 39:244-248 (July 11, 1980). Helen Schmierer's definition, quoted in note 5, p. 2 of this volume is more narrow.

2.   Charles A. Cutter, *Rules for a Dictionary Catalog,* 4th ed., rewritten, U.S. Bureau of Education, Special Report on Public Libraries, Pt. II (Washington, D.C.: Government Printing Office, 1904), 12.

3.   International Conference on Cataloging Principles, Paris, 1961, *Report* (London: International Federation of Library Associations, 1963), 91-92.

4.   Helen F. Schmierer, "The Relationship of Authority Control to the Library Catalog," *Illinois Libraries* 62:599-603 (September 1980).

5.   Ibid., 600.

6.   Ritvars Bregzis, "The Syndetic Structure of the Catalog" in *Authority Control: The Key to Tomorrow's Catalog,* ed. Mary W. Ghikas (Phoenix, Ariz.: Oryx Press, 1979), 19-35.

7.   Michael Gorman, "Authority Files in a Developed Machine System (With Particular Reference to AACR II)," in *What's in a Name: Control of Catalogue Records through Automated Authority Files,* ed. and comp. Natsuko Y. Furuya (Toronto: University of Toronto Press, 1978).

8.   Bregzis, "The Syndetic Structure of the Catalog."

9.   Larry Auld, "Authority Control: An Eighty-Year Review," *Library Resources and Technical Services* 26:319-330 (October/December 1982).

10.   Ibid.

11.   Ibid.

12.   Ibid.

13.   Ibid., 320.

14.   Ibid.

15.   Ibid., 321.

16.   Ibid., 320.

17.   Dorcas Fellows, *Cataloging Rules with Explanations and Illustrations,* 2nd ed. (New York: H. W. Wilson, 1922), 273-279.

18.   Ibid., 273.

19.   Ibid., 274.

20.   Auld, "Authority Control: An Eighty-Year Review."

2

CREATING AUTHORITY RECORDS AND IMPLEMENTING AUTHORITY SYSTEMS

CREATING AUTHORITY RECORDS AS PART OF THE CATALOGING PROCESS

In *simple* terms, the creation of an authority record is prompted by the cataloging of an item representing a work the author or the title of which (in the case of works lacking authors) is not yet represented in the local catalog or in the universe of bibliographic data accessible to the cataloger.[1] The choice of the terms *work* and *item* here is deliberate. A work is an abstract concept related to access points. An item is a physical manifestation of the work, a concrete object described in the catalog. Specifically, an authority record is created for each new entry or access point[2] used in a catalog.

An individual authority record consists of several parts. Depending on the individual library, it includes a heading, cross-references to the heading, notes on the creation of the heading, and other important data relevant to the heading. The authority record may also include related headings as well as control numbers, the name of the person who prepared the record, the date of preparation, the call number of the first bibliographic item with that access point, and other locally mandated information. Unlike bibliographic records, there is no standard code like AACR2 for the formation of the content of authority records.

Cataloging and Authority Work

In order to understand the role and purpose of the authority record in bibliographic control, it must be viewed as part of the cataloging process. The following list briefly describes the four major steps involved in cataloging, showing where authority work and the individual authority record fit in: (1) bibliographic description; (2) choice of access points; (3) form of access points; and (4) subject analysis. For our purposes the assignment of subject headings and classification will be viewed under the rubric of subject analysis.

Bibliographic description results from the application of relevant portions of a cataloging code and the International Standard Bibliographic Description (ISBD) in such a way as to produce a standardized systematic description of the item being cataloged. In rule 1.0B AACR2 describes a maximum of eight areas in the formulation of a bibliographic description: (1) title and statement of responsibility; (2) edition; (3) material (or type of publication) specific details; (4) publication, distribution, etc.; (5) physical description; (6) series; (7) notes; and (8) standard number and terms of availability.[3]

The description formed by the cataloger's interpretation of the item cataloged and the use of the rules for description in force at the time constitute the bibliographic description of the item. This is, in effect, a surrogate of the item described. One or more copies of this surrogate are then placed in a catalog and used to locate in the library the item that the surrogate represents.

In order to find the surrogate in the catalog, however, it is necessary to choose access points by which the item can be found and which will determine the appearance of the surrogate in one or more places of the catalog or store of bibliographic information. Choice of access points, then, is the second major step in cataloging. The choice of access points is also prescribed by cataloging codes, based on the concept of intellectual or artistic responsibility (authorship) for the work of which the item is a manifestation. In order to maximize the retrievability of the surrogate (the bibliographic description), and also to minimize the cost of processing, storing, and maintaining the cataloging information, cataloging codes restrict the choice of access points by giving strict criteria for making such choices. For example, translators of works are chosen as access points only if they meet certain criteria. Rule 21.30K1 of the presently used cataloging code in North America, AACR2, reads:

> 21.30K1. Translators. Make an added entry under the heading for a translator if the main entry is under the heading for a corporate body or under title.
>
> If the main entry is under the heading for a person, make an added entry under the heading for a translator if:
>
> 1.   the translation is in verse
>   or
>
> 2.   the translation is important in its own right
>   or
>
> 3.   the work has been translated into the same language more than once
>   or
>
> 4.   the wording of the chief source of information suggests that the translator is the author
>   or
>
> 5.   the main entry heading may be difficult for catalogue users to find (e.g., as with many oriental and medieval works).[4]

Note the mixture of objective (1, 3, 4) and subjective (2, 5) criteria.

Up to this point the cataloger has only had to deal with two different documents. One is the bibliographic item to be cataloged; the other is the cataloging code, as interpreted by the institution, network, and national library. With these two items bibliographic description and choice of entry can be carried out without reference to any other information. But as the third step in the cataloging process is begun, the cataloger is suddenly brought face to face with an entire universe of bibliographic information, or at least a universe of access points that will alter the decision made about the form of the particular access point chosen in step two. The determination of the form of access point can be a very complicated process in itself. The present cataloging code can be used as an example. Chapters 22 through 25 of AACR2 deal with determining forms of access points. There are separate chapters for the various types of names formed: personal names (Chapter 22), geographic names (Chapter 23), corporate names (Chapter 24), and uniform titles (Chapter 25). For each of these there are several rules for determining the proper form of name. Once this form is chosen by the cataloger for a particular item, several questions arise, all relating to a speculative concern of the cataloger. The speculation is: This name may appear again in conjunction with another work cataloged in the library. It is possible that the next time this name is subjected to the rules in force for cataloging, the same form of name will not be prescribed. This will cause problems in the catalog (as we saw in Chapter 1), impairing its finding and gathering functions. What is needed is a mechanism for recording such decisions, as well as other information relevant to the decision. This mechanism is the authority record. Let us now turn to a consideration of the authority record and the different types of data contained in it.

TYPES OF AUTHORITY DATA

Several different types of authority data may be found on an authority record: headings (personal names, corporate and conference names, geographic names, uniform titles, series or serials [as a special case of uniform title], and combinations of names and titles such as "Beethoven, Ludwig van, Symphony No. 5"), references, notes, and application and treatment instructions, as well as locally mandated information (cataloger's initials, call number of work cataloged, etc.).

Headings

An authorized heading is that form of access point prescribed by the current set of cataloging rules and the situation in the local catalog. Authority records are set up to record headings, as well as information about them, so that the headings may be used uniformly in the catalog or machine-readable bibliographic file. The heading is a name or title that has already been chosen as an access point for a particular bibliographic record. As we saw in Chapter 1, this choice of access point takes place prior to the formation of an authority record. An authority record cannot be made unless the heading recorded in it has been chosen as an access point for a bibliographic record. Once this decision is made, the next group of decisions that faces the cataloger concerns the form that the heading chosen as an access point will take.

This chosen form is called the heading, the authorized heading, the authorized form, the standard form, or the uniform standard heading. It can be different from the form of the name or title that appears in the publication. It can include additions to the name, such as dates or titles. It can be in inverted order or in a different language, include a qualifier, or be a different name altogether (in the form of a pseudonym). In short, the heading may not resemble at all the form that appears in the publication. The authority record is the tool that guides the user from the form found in a publication to the form appearing on the bibliographic record as an access point.[5] These headings, or authorized access points, can be of several different types: personal names, corporate and conference names, geographic names, uniform titles, and series. Such headings can also include subject headings, but such material is beyond the scope of this book except where the categories of headings named above serve as subject headings.

One axiom of authority work that has already been emphasized is that the purpose of an authority record is to record the authorized heading. This authorized heading is created, insofar as possible, to be unique. Therefore, in discussing personal names, as well as other types of headings, it is useful to recall the origins of such headings and the ways in which such headings can be made unique. In some cases this may seem like belaboring the obvious, but the exercise will, I believe, help underline a principle that is operative in all authority work and that is at the heart of authority systems: uniqueness of heading.

Personal Names

It will not surprise anyone to hear that personal names, for the most part, are given at birth. This simple-minded fact can, however, point out some problems with the creation of authorized headings, as well as some devices for making a name different from a similar name—i.e., making it unique.

The birth name is the choice of someone other than the person named. As the person matures and develops an individual personality, he or she may begin to dislike the birth name or feel obliged to change it for political, social, or racial reasons. If that person becomes an author and decides that a changed name, different form of name, or pseudonym will appear on the title page of his or her publication, then the cataloger, or person preparing the authority record, will have to choose between the name on the publication and the full name of the person at birth, if such information is available. The rules that govern the form of personal name chosen are found in Chapter 22 of AACR2.

So personal names may change for some of the reasons outlined above, as well as others. Once a proper form of name is chosen by the cataloger, however, one additional step is faced. Is the form of name chosen unique within the known bibliographic universe?[6] If it is not unique, then some addition to the name must be made if at all possible. Here is where the birth date, for example, comes in. There may be two men by the name of William Morris, but if one was born in 1834 and the other in 1962, the addition of this information to the names, as part of the authorized form, will make each entry unique.

Some other peculiarities with regard to personal names bear mention. For example, William Morris, who was born in 1834, does not appear in the catalog as William Morris, 1834-1896, but as Morris, William, 1834-1896. Inversion is another way of standardizing and finding personal names. (In some languages [e.g., Chinese, Hungarian] the family name appears first [e.g., Kaldor Emre].) For many languages, alphabetized lists of names are arranged by surname. Hence the authorized form of name appears in inverted order, in order to follow this convention. Another example: After the Roman Empire expanded to include much of Europe, the names of many authors began to appear in a Latin form and in vernacular language forms (e.g., Ioannes, Johann, Jean, John). Which form should be used in the heading? These and other questions are asked and answered in order to provide an orderly list of names for retrieval. The rules for carrying out this task try to meet the conventional expectations of users of catalogs. That they do so to such a great degree is to their, and the rulemakers', credit.

To sum up, then, personal names can undergo many changes from the initial birth name. Names are legally changed, pseudonyms are used, titles are assumed, and people marry, sometimes taking different names or forming new, hyphenated names. Behind this onomastic jungle lies one person. At the time of cataloging, or creation of an authority record, the cataloger determines the one form that will be used, or—in the usual exception to any cataloging rule—the minimal number of forms, if pseudonyms are involved. Each form identifies a bibliographic identity (one person may have multiple bibliographic identities, each one of which is to be identified by a standard form). The other forms not used are name variants for that one human being or bibliographic being, and these variants play a role in the authority record as references.

To make a name unique many techniques are used, involving the addition of birth and/or death dates, expansion to the fullest form of name available, and in some cases addition of a phrase denoting the subject matter of the author, if this helps to make the personal name unique. There are several pitfalls involved in using subject matter, however: authors may change their interests, and such phrases are subjective and may not provide useful information. The many ways in which personal names change and the ways in which they are made unique provide endless amusement, as well as frustration, for the creators of authority records.

Corporate and Conference Names

Corporate names, whose definition includes conference names, are those applied to any corporate body—any group of persons that has organized for a particular activity. The definition given by AACR2 is more precise, but just as broad:

> Corporate body. An organization or group of persons that is identified by a particular name and that acts, or may act, as an entity. Typical examples of corporate bodies are associations, institutions, business firms, nonprofit enterprises, governments, government agencies, religious bodies, local churches, and conferences.[7]

Corporate names, like personal names, come into existence when the body itself is created. Unlike personal names, however, corporate name changes occur with much more rapidity and for different reasons, and hence are treated differently by cataloging codes. Furthermore, corporate bodies can survive indefinitely. The longer lifespan of such entities provides a greater potential for change. When a corporate body changes its name, it is usually because of changes in purpose or scope of the activities of the body itself.

I am not attempting to give any hard and fast rules in this area, but simply to describe the differences between personal and corporate names. When the Institute of Scientific and Technical Information (Institut nauchno-tekhnicheskoi informatsii) in Moscow changed its name to the All-Union Institute of Scientific and Technical Information (Vsesoiuznyi institut nauchno-tekhnicheskoi informatsii) in 1955, the name change signified a change in scope—the institute would now have broader, national responsibilities. Because of the change in scope, the corporate body itself changed in a measurable way. Because this kind of change in purpose or scope is and has been perceived as a fundamental change in the corporate body itself, the current cataloging code treats each change of name as constituting the demise of one organization and the birth of another, which is identified by a different and unique name, not a name variant of a single unchanged entity. As a result, when a corporate body changes its name, in the eyes of the authority record maker one more corporate body now exists. This newly formed body is related to its predecessor, but it is fundamentally different, different enough to warrant a separate authority record and a different authorized heading. (The same principle is at work here as in dealing with serial title changes.) Another complicating factor for corporate names is the existence of subordinate headings for corporate bodies within corporate bodies. The ways in which such related bodies and subordinate bodies are linked through authority records are discussed in the References and Notes sections below.

Once a specific form or name of a corporate body is chosen as an authorized heading, the cataloger faces the same dilemma as was the case with personal names: Is this name unique? If the cataloger ascertains that it is not unique, then just as with personal names, additions or qualifications must be made to the name to identify it clearly and provide a means for distinguishing it from other names identical to it. One way this is done is by adding a qualifier, which can consist of another corporate body to which the one in question is subordinate or some geographic name. For example, Institute of Geology is a perfectly good name for a corporate body. But is this the Institute of Geology that is part of the Academy of Sciences or is it the Institute of Geology that is part of the Scripps Institution? The addition of the name of the parent body will distinguish one from the other. Do we wish to find the Australian Society of Abstractors or the American? Again, the addition of the qualifier can provide this name with the character of uniqueness.

Conference names are considered corporate names. Conference names are mentioned separately because there are more ways of qualifying them to make them unique. Three possible pieces of information may be added: the number of the meeting (if it was numbered), the date on which the meeting was held, and the place it was held. A conference name such as Conference on the Vivisection of Terminally Ill Frogs can be identified as "Conference on the Vivisection of Terminally Ill Frogs (3rd : 1957 : Bronxville, N.Y.)." The qualifiers serve to distinguish this conference from the one held in Finley, North Dakota, in 1964, which was the sixth such meeting. Because of the nature of conferences, whose names remain the same but whose qualifiers change, conferences fall in the middle of the continuum between personal names and corporate names. Under the current cataloging rules, the addition of these qualifiers is mandatory if the information is readily available, even if the name of the meeting itself is unique. This is an example of predictive cataloging.

Geographic Names

Geographic names have caused much confusion in cataloging circles because such names can be the official names of governments or governmental jurisdictions and therefore, in essence and in practice, corporate bodies. Geographic names can also, of course, be the names of regions or areas.

According to present conventions, when a geographic name is used in a subject heading and the name is not intended to be the corporate name of the political jurisdiction, or when the geographic name is used as a subdivision, then the latest name of that geographic entity is used. So, for example, the term Soviet Union would be used to subdivide the subject heading Education, even if the subject covered in the publication was education in prerevolutionary Russia.

If, however, a corporate body, say, the Ministry of Internal Affairs of Imperial Russia, were to be designated in a heading, then the term "Russia. Ministerstvo vnutrennykh del" would be used, since the geographic name here functions as a corporate body.

As with personal and corporate names, geographic names change, or the entities that they designate split into other areas, or the area designated by a geographic name merges or joins with another to form a new one. The authority record, under the vigilant eye of the cataloger, reflects these changes and other sometimes bizarre and incestuous relationships.

Uniform Titles

Uniform titles are used when a single work is identified by more than one title. The uniform title is the standard identification for the work and is the form to which variants are referred. This somewhat metaphysical definition will become clear by example.

Suppose that a work is issued in German and translated into a number of other languages. Should the work be known by the original German title, one of the translated titles, or all the titles? Again, we rely on convention by affirming uniqueness and by choosing one variant to which the others refer. In the case of translations of modern works, the original title is chosen as the uniform title and the translated titles are used as cross-references to it. In certain cases of early publications, however, the translated title has become better known than the original, and the more familiar title is chosen as the uniform title. As with the other headings we have considered so far, there occasionally arise examples of identical titles that are not titles of the same work. The cataloger is then forced to qualify the uniform title in some way to make it unique. This is done by adding such things as dates of composition, form subheadings, and similar devices.

Series or Serials

The titles of series or serials are a special case of uniform title. They are special because the title for a serial can have special relationships with other serials, such as chronological or hierarchical relationships, as well as special relationships with corporate bodies, personal names, and geographic names.[8] Titles of series or serials must be made unique, just like other headings. The means by which this is done varies with the case at hand, but some common devices include qualifying the title with the name of the corporate body that issued the series or with the name of the place in which it was produced (for newspapers, for example), or preceding or following the title with the name of the superseries or subseries to which it is related.

References

References are the second major part of the authority record. Generally speaking, references, or reference tracings, are alternate forms or variant forms of the authorized heading. Moreover, reference tracings can also be related headings that bear a special relationship to the authorized heading. These are known as *see also from* references. The rules for forming references, what constitutes a valid reference, and the general guidelines for forming references are given in Chapter 26 of the AACR2.

An authority record does not have to contain a reference to be an authority record. On the other hand, there can be many references for one heading. Extreme cases have been observed in which as many as fifty references have been made to the authorized form of the heading.[9]

In card-based systems, cross-references are usually indicated below the main, or authorized, heading and are preceded by the letter x or s denoting cross-reference or *see from* reference. When a *see also from* reference is made, xx is used. So in a card-based system, the authority card could look like Figure 2.1.

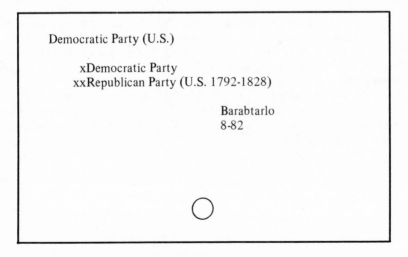

Figure 2.1. Authority card with cross-references.

Notes

Notes are used on authority records to carry out a variety of tasks. For example, they can be used to indicate the sources checked in creating the authority record and the results of that search. They can give background information about the heading in order to make clear its relationship to other headings or to give some history about the development of the heading. On authority cards, notes are usually kept to a minimum because of the limited space for such information. In machine-readable records, however, there seems to be a more permissive spirit at work, and notes on authority cards can become lengthy. Take, for example, this lengthy note about the Communist Party of America:

> The Left Wing Section of the Socialist Party was organized in July 1919; in Sept. it split into the Communist Party of America and the Communist Labor Party of America. In May 1920 the Communist Labor Party of America united with a section of the Communist Party of America to form the United Communist Party of America. In 1921 the United Communist Party of America and the remainder of the Communist Party of America merged to form the Workers Party of America. The name was changed in 1925 to Workers (Communist) Party of America; and in 1929 to Communist Party of the United States of America. In May 1944 the Communist Party of the United States of America disbanded and was replaced by the Communist Political Association. In 1945 it was re-created as an active political party. Works by the Workers Party of America, the Workers (Communist) Party of America, and the Communist Party of the United States of America are found under Communist Party of the United States of America. Works by the other bodies are found under the name used at the time of publication.[10]

Application and Treatment Instructions and Other Information

In some institutions, information about how the heading has been applied is also contained on the authority record. Such notes are usually confined to series. For example, the authority card might indicate whether the chosen series heading was classified separately or as a collection, whether the series was analyzed, and other information about the series itself.[11]

In addition, the name of the cataloger, the date the authority record was prepared, and the cataloging code used to formulate the heading, along with the call number of the publication that prompted the creation of the authority, may be found on authority records.

SOURCES FOR AUTHORITY DATA

For the individual library, the sources of authority data can be many and varied. One of the best ways to discover and examine these sources is to trace the cataloging and authority-making process in a typical library.

Once the cataloger has chosen a name or title as an access point, he or she must follow a labyrinth of processing to discover what further work has to be done to establish the form of name. This may seem an extreme way to put it, but remember that the following possibilities exist:

1. the chosen access point has already been processed by the Library of Congress and catalogers there have created the authorized form of name

2. a library that contributes bibliographic records to the same network to which our hypothetical library belongs has already created the authorized form for the heading

3. the library itself has already chosen the authorized form of the heading and it already exists in the library's authority file

4. various combinations of the above

5. none of the above

If any of possibilities 1 through 4 apply, the cataloger must rely on local policy to determine which form of heading takes priority over the others. An additional complicating factor may arise if, say, the library had created its own form of heading and subsequently the Library of Congress established the form differently. For the moment, however, let us examine preexisting authorized forms as one source for authority data.

Library of Congress Authority Records

Once each week the Library of Congress issues in machine-readable form new and updated authority records that were created in the preceding week. These records are also distributed quarterly in microfiche form. The machine-readable records are purchased by the primary networks and made available to members of those networks for use. (It must be remembered that the authority files available for use through the primary networks may differ somewhat from the original issue of the Library of Congress.) The headings reflected in these authority records are used by the Library of Congress in its current cataloging. So libraries may rely on the copies of LC authority records themselves, their manifestations in primary networks, or solely on the authorized heading as reflected in currently produced bibliographic records. Most libraries follow the LC-produced authority records when they are available, since a large part of their current cataloging is produced by the Library of Congress. If they follow LC records closely, then no changes need to be made in the bibliographic records produced by the Library of Congress and subsequently used by libraries, either in card form or available via the networks.

Headings on Records of Contributing Libraries

Another source of authority data are the bibliographic records produced by libraries that belong to a primary network. Although authority records themselves are not available from these libraries, the form of heading chosen by them is available. Some libraries also belong to the Name Authority Cooperative (NACO) Project. (See also Chapter 6, p. 68.) These libraries contribute authority records to the Library of Congress, and the records are then distributed as LC authority records.

The Existing Library Authority File

The most obvious source for authority data is the library's authority file. If a chosen heading already has an authority record, and that authority record does not conflict with current LC practice, the cataloger does not have to search further.

If, however, none of the above-mentioned sources produces the required name or title, then the cataloger is thrown back on the cataloging code itself and the publication at hand as a starting point for choosing the proper form of name. When this occurs, the cataloging code, the publication at hand, and assorted reference works form the triad of sources and decision-making guidelines out of which comes the authorized heading.

The Cataloging Code as a Tool for Standardization

The cataloging code is designed to standardize bibliographic description and forms of headings so that both bibliographic and authority records may be exchanged and used in a mutually trustworthy environment. The assumption is that, given a clearly written code and adequately trained catalogers, the same authorized heading will be obtained for an access point by all catalogers who attempt it, even if the people establishing the headings never communicate. Such consistency does occur, but cataloging data, or rather the raw material out of which cataloging data comes, is sometimes so ambiguous that consistency is not achieved. This phenomenon of inconsistency has prompted Jesse Shera to issue the two laws of cataloging: "1. One cataloger will never accept the work of another cataloger. 2. A cataloger will not accept his/her own work six months after it has been done."[12]

To further complicate the issue, the Library of Congress issues what are called rule interpretations, or RIs, which are glosses on the liturgical text, so to speak. These interpretations either expand on and give further guidance to rules in the code itself, or announce the preference of one alternate rule over another, or in some instances (e.g., microfilms) contradict the rules. These two documents, then, serve to provide guidelines for standardization of authority data.[13]

The Publication Itself

The publication being cataloged is the primary source of authority data. But for some materials, notably music and sound recordings, other sources are frequently used. Of course, the most predominant place where authority information can be found is the title page or chief source of information.[14] There are, however, other parts of the publication where related information is sometimes hidden. These places may include the verso of the title page, where the original title of a translation is sometimes printed. The colophon, at least in Soviet and East European works, often carries the full form of the name of the person whose abbreviated first name and patronymic appear on the title page. The series statement can appear, and has appeared, virtually anywhere in the publication. Often a preface or foreword will include some historical or biographical information about a corporate body or person chosen as an access point. Finally, the text of the publication itself can provide such information as birth and death dates, use of pseudonyms, and other data that are the result of previous research and may not be found elsewhere.

Reference Books as Sources of Authority Data

Reference books are reliable sources for authority data, but the most obvious ones are frequently overlooked. They include encyclopedias, bibliographies, bio-bibliographies, biographical dictionaries, and atlases. Some reference books serve as intermediaries to the source data sought. Indexes of book reviews, newspapers, and other finding tools can lead to sources that give abundant authority information. I will not here attempt to describe the many ways that reference books can provide authority data. Reference work is a subdiscipline of librarianship in its own right. But one of the engaging aspects of authority work is its kinship to reference work. Such linkages among subdisciplines can help to break down the psychological and administrative barriers that separate these fields. The increase in communication between catalogers and reference librarians because of this is to be applauded.

CREATING THE AUTHORITY RECORD

The cataloger records the information he or she is gathering on some kind of work sheet. Such a sheet may be highly formalized, such as that used by NACO Project participants, or a 3x5 slip. Once all the information is collected, the next step is to create the authority record itself. This usually entails the arrangement of the information gathered into some kind of prescribed form, whether it be a prescribed position on a 3x5 card or definition and identification by a machine-readable tag and appropriate subfield codes.

Card-based Authority Systems

There is no nationally prescribed method or format for transcribing authority data onto cards, but several conventions are widely used. The first and major convention is the placement of the authorized heading at the top of the card, in the same form as it would and does appear on catalog cards. Below this cross-references are placed. *See from* references are indicated by the prefix x and *see also from* references are indicated by the prefix xx. Below this any notes are given. Finally the name or initials of the cataloger, the date the record was prepared, and the call number or title of the publication that prompted the preparation of the authority card is given. (See Figure 2.2.)

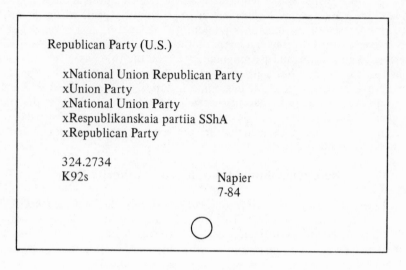

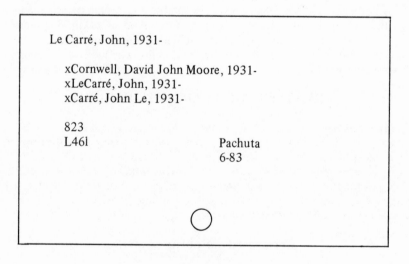

Figure 2.2. Examples of card-based authority cards.

The name of the cataloger is given not, as a cynic might suggest, to allow the cataloger to be nailed to the wall if a mistake is discovered—although doubtless it has occasionally been used for this purpose. Rather, the name is noted so that if questions concerning the authority record should arise, the questioner will know to whom to direct the inquiry. The date is given so that if in the future a heading should come to seem bizarre or simply wrong, the time of establishment may provide a clue to deciphering the puzzle. It could be that at the time in question a certain rule interpretation was in force that was subsequently withdrawn. One final, minor point: The authority record need not consist of just one card. If the cross-references are numerous enough, or the notes lengthy enough, several cards may be used to contain all the appropriate information.

Machine-based Authority Systems

There is a prescribed format for machine-readable authority records. Published in 1981, it is called *Authorities: A MARC Format,* first edition. (A preliminary edition was issued in 1976.) The format the first edition recommends is the one in which authority records in machine systems are communicated. The Appendix to this book describes the format in depth and explains the various fields and the information contained in them. Suffice it to say at this point that machine-readable authority records contain the same categories of information as do card-based authority records. They also contain other information relevant to the processing of the machine-readable record. Figure 2.3 (pp. 26-27) shows the work form used by LC and NACO Project participants to create machine-readable authority records.

(Text continues on p. 28.)

| NAME AUTHORITY | | To NACO ☐ | To Subj. Cat. ☐ |

040 (CAS)	001 (CRD)	s = Surname	f = Forename
		c = Corporate body	m = Meeting
_____‡DLC	ₙ84- 047946	u = Uniform title heading	g = Geographic
26. Revision Cat. (Date/Code)	1XX (NA) HEADING		

FIXED FIELDS

6.	b	GM
7.	c d	Rules
8.	b	Non-unique name
9.	b	Memo
	c	Provisional
	d	Preliminary
11.		Heading not in LC
12.	a	Evaluation of references
29	c d	Cataloging source

25. Original Cat.(Date/Code)   note (temp. info.)

67C (NWC) SOURCES FOUND

952 Cataloger's perm. note

675 (NSI) SOURCES NOT FOUND

969 Short term temp. note

667 (NUN) NOTE (perm. info.)

053 (CLA) CLASSIFICATION NUMBER

.6-128a (rev 9/83)

Figure 2.3. Work form used by LC and NACO Project participants to create machine-readable authority records.

DISTRIBUTION SYMBOLS

AUTHORITY	965 (DOA)		NEZ												
REFERENCE	960 (DOR)	AOC	MCL	AMU	ASR	M	AM	ACN	HE	AJ	AK	AL	NE	SA	

Control data					Cataloger-generated reference (stapled)	

Spec rel code	Tracing use	Rules a	dn a	cg b	4XX (XE) SEE REFERENCE
n	n				‡
n	n				
n	n				
n	n				
n	n				
n	n				
n	n				
n	n				
n	n				
n	n				

el a	lr b	Tracing use b	Rules	dn a	cg c	5XX (XO) SEE ALSO REFERENCE
			n			‡
			n			
			n			
			n			
			n			
			n			

Notes (temp. info.)		Id/Date
	MARC Ed Received	
	Input	
	Reviewed/checked	
	Verified	

Figure 2.3–*Continued*

CREATING THE AUTHORITY FILE

In a basic sense, the most direct way of creating an authority file is to take a bunch of authority records and arrange them according to an accepted alphabetization or collation scheme. Presto! You have an authority file. This is essentially what is done, but it is not quite so simple. Remember that at this point I am simply talking about the creation of a file of authority records, not about any type of linkage to bibliographic files. This will be taken up in Chapter 3.

Some basic factors should be taken into account when creating the file—factors that have little to do with authorities as such, but have a lot to do with intelligent administration. For the present, let us ignore machine-based authority files and concentrate on card-based files.

First, there must be a place to store the authority file. This place must be accessible to all who use the file and those who maintain it. The file will grow with time, so enough room must be allocated to house it as it expands. Proper storage drawers, normally catalog card drawers, should be used to keep the file as orderly and neat as possible for long-term use. The file site will receive heavy traffic, since catalogers will consult the file, and filers will file into the file, and catalog maintenance personnel will maintain the file.

Second, there must be staff members whose chief responsibility is to maintain the file by typing cross-references, filing into the file, correcting obvious errors, etc. This aspect of authority work is frequently overlooked in the initial stages of planning, much to everyone's chagrin later on.

Third, there must be policies in effect that govern the creation of the authority records and the authority file and the procedures or routines to which catalogers and others engaged in the establishment of authority data must adhere. This last item requires some discussion. What should be the policy for the creation of authority records and authority files?

Local Policy for Authority Work

Local policy for authority work should consist of at least four facets:

1.   the prescribed format for authority records (which has already been discussed)

2.   the assignment of a different rank to each external source of authority records, and the different procedures to be followed with various sources

3.   the extent to which cross-references are to be made in given situations

4.   how to handle names that are the same as, or similar to, other names

As we have seen above, any library can receive authority data from many sources. There are LC authority records and locally made authority records, as well as established headings that have been used in bibliographic records. A crucial aspect of policy focuses on the importance of each of these sources relative to each other.

For example, let us take a typical situation in the life of a cataloger to illustrate how an established policy is necessary for guidance. Let us assume that the cataloger has at hand a recently published book and a printout from one of the primary networks. The cataloger can discern from the printout that the record was issued by the Library of Congress and that AACR2 was used for the bibliographic description and the formation of headings. The first question asked by the cataloger is: Should I accept the form of heading as it appears on the record? If the answer to this is yes, a subsequent question is: Does the form of heading on the record already exist in our local authority file? This necessitates the examination of the local file. If the heading on the record and the heading in the local file coincide, all is well, for now at least. What happens, however, if the cataloger searches the on-line authority file that is supposed to contain LC authorized headings and the heading there is different from the heading on the bibliographic record, or if there is no heading in the on-line file?

Other complications could occur in a different scenario. What happens if the bibliographic record is not formulated by the Library of Congress, or if the heading on the bibliographic record, even though it is an LC heading, does not match the local authority file? It is easy to see that a general, clearly written library policy must be in force to guide the cataloger through the various decisions to be made during the course of cataloging. One way to formulate the policy is to assign a priority or rank to the various sources. This way, if there is a conflict between two sources, the policy will prescribe the choice, with instructions on what to do next. Or the policy could be less rigid and give some discretion to the cataloger.

Along with the "what to do now" problem come choices about the number and type of cross-references to be made. Guidance is given in Chapter 26 of AACR2 and the LC rule interpretations. These rules, however, are highly ambiguous and confusing. Local policy must be more specific and should combine instructions for cross-references with the priority instructions. Should a cross-reference be made, for example, from a heading in a local library authority file when it is superseded by an LC authority record? Should all the cross-references that were contained in that local authority record become cross-references to the new local authority record, after it is changed to conform to the LC record?

One minor aspect of authority policy is to determine how to handle names that are the same as, or similar to, other names. One example is that of the two Irish writers, Patrick Kavanagh (whose middle initial is J.) and P. J. Kavanagh (whose first name is Patrick). One way of doing this best is to include a note to the effect: "Do not confuse with Smith, Adam, author of *Wealth of Nations*," or some similar qualification such as birth and death dates.

Some of the problems inherent in the card-based system also exist in machine-based systems. There must be a clear authority policy similar, if not identical to, the type suggested for the card-based system. The act of changing bibliographic records whose headings have been changed in an authority file can, in some systems, be done much more easily than in card-based systems. But since some of the problems related to creating the file are inherent in the nature of technology itself, we will defer discussion of these problems to Chapter 3, under the rubric of links to the bibliographic file, and to Chapter 5, where examples of machine-based systems are discussed.

NOTES

1.   In some large systems, a cataloger will have access to bibliographic records not contained in the local catalog.

2.   The term *access point* has not yet been rigorously defined.

3.   Michael Gorman and Paul Winkler, eds., *Anglo-American Cataloguing Rules,* 2nd ed. (Chicago: ALA, 1978), 13.

4.   Ibid., 324.

5.   I will discuss access points from the point of view of a displayed bibliographic record, whether that record is a catalog card or an image on a cathode-ray tube.

6.   One can, of course, only deal with the known bibliographic universe, which consists of one's own catalog and others that are widely available (e.g., NUC, OCLC, RLIN). Predictive cataloging attempts to deal with potential conflicts with catalogs not available to the cataloger and headings that will be created in the future. The most common example of predictive cataloging is the addition of dates to names not in conflict in the known bibliographic universe.

7.   Gorman and Winkler, eds., *Anglo-American Cataloguing Rules,* 2nd ed., 565.

8.   Michael Gorman and Robert H. Burger, "Serial Control in a Developed Machine System," *Serials Librarian* 5(1):13-26 (Spring 1982).

9.   See, for example, Library of Congress Authority Record n-79106441, dealing with the Council of Mutual Economic Assistance (CMEA).

10.   LC Authority Record n-79036120, for Communist Party of the United States of America.

11.   See notes 640-646 in *Authorities: A MARC Format,* and pp. 110-111 in this volume.

12.   Cited in Lawrence E. Leonard, *Inter-Indexer Consistency Studies: 1954-1975: A Review of the Literature and Summary of Study Results* (University of Illinois Graduate School of Library Science Occasional Paper 131), 1.

13.   These rule interpretations are initially issued only to LC catalogers. Once each quarter, RIs issued since the previous compilation are gathered, edited, and published for national use in LC's *Cataloging Service Bulletin.*

14.   *Chief source of information* is defined in *Anglo-American Cataloguing Rules,* 2nd ed., 564, as "the source of bibliographic data to be given first preference as the source from which a bibliographic description (or portion thereof) is prepared." The chief source can be different for different types of publications. For printed monographs the chief source is the title page; for a machine-readable data file with an adequate internal user label, it is the label. Each area of description has a prescribed source of information. This source may be the same as the chief source for the type of publication. If the prescribed source does not contain the information, but the information is available elsewhere, it must be enclosed in brackets in the bibliographic description of the item to indicate its less-than-reliable nature. For example, the prescribed source of information for series in printed monographs is the whole publication, but for title and statement of responsibility it is the title page only.

3

THE USE AND MAINTENANCE
OF AUTHORITY SYSTEMS

The title of this chapter may need a vigorous defense. After all, it might be argued, authority systems are made to use, and if one understands how the system is made, then the use of it is almost beside the point. The necessity for maintaining authority systems might also be questioned. If the cataloging rules are followed at the time of cataloging and the correct form of name chosen, what maintenance could possibly be needed?

But authority systems are used by more people than catalogers and, depending on the system, by more than the library staff. Furthermore, the dynamism of authority systems requires that the systems be maintained, if for no other reason than to control the dynamism and prevent the system from becoming dysfunctional. Dysfunction would result if no changes were made; the headings would go out of date and retrieval of items would be hampered.

USERS OF AUTHORITY FILES

The Cataloger

Catalogers are the primary users of authority files in card-based systems. The cataloger creates the authority file and, in the process of later cataloging, uses that file to determine if a given heading has already been used and what form that heading takes.[1] The cataloger uses the authority file first of all as a precedent file, to determine if an authorized decision has already been made about a heading chosen as an access point. Secondly, the cataloger can use the authority file as a model for constructing similar headings. In some cases, the authority file will contain a form of a name that is highly unusual but that has been prescribed for that particular name. The cataloger, providing he or she has a good memory, will use that heading as a model for others. In the course of using the authority file as a source of precedents, the cataloger will also determine if, given the latest evidence at hand about a particular heading, the existing authority record needs to be changed. Such changing of authority data will be discussed in more detail below.

Acquisitions Personnel

The authority file is also used by acquisitions personnel in ordering materials for the library. Often a name appearing in a publisher's catalog or in a request by a user may not be verified, and the librarian ordering the item may need to do some additional bibliographic work to determine if the library already has the item requested, in which case it may or may not be ordered, depending on local policy. Further, once the name is verified, accurate bibliographic information can be passed on to the vendor or book supplier, thereby avoiding time-consuming correspondence between vendor and library and excessively long waiting time on the part of the requestor. On the other hand, the "full" or "correct" name may actually be unfamiliar, and thus misleading, to a vendor or supplier. The utility and cost efficiency of bibliographic searching by acquisitions librarians is still being debated.

Reference Librarians

Reference librarians use the authority file in ways similar to acquisitions librarians. When a reference librarian receives an inquiry, one of the many tools to which he or she turns is the catalog and its associated apparatus. Effective use of the catalog leads to the use of the authority file. Again, the request received may use a form of name that is obsolete, a pseudonym, or some other uncommon variant. In order to find out whether the library has what the patron is requesting, the reference librarian may use the authority file to determine if the name requested is a valid form of name in the local catalog, and if not, what variant form is used.[2]

The Public

The public patrons of the library may use the authority file as a reference or finding aid for the catalog itself, in much the same way as the reference librarian uses it. In some libraries, of course, the authority file is not accessible to the public, or if it is, the public may not know of its existence. In machine-based catalogs, the authority file may be working on the patron's behalf without the knowledge of the patron. The level of interaction with the authority file by the patron, as well as by other noncataloging personnel, depends on the library as well as on the type of link the authority file has to the bibliographic file.[3]

LINKS TO THE BIBLIOGRAPHIC FILE

The authority file is used, as we have seen, as a record of decisions about forms of headings to be used on catalog records. This fact alone creates an implicit linkage between the authority file and the bibliographic file. The way this linkage is made explicit, however, is determined by the types of linkages possible. There are four types of relationships between authority files and bibliographic files in effect today:

1. authority file completely independent of bibliographic file

2. authority file "coordinated" with bibliographic file

3. authority file existing as part of the bibliographic file

4. authority file in direct electronic connection with the bibliographic file

Authority File Independent of Bibliographic File

Probably the least desirable relationship of the authority file to the bibliographic file is that of complete independence of each other. Although it may seem surprising that such an arrangement would exist at all, there are two systems that have such a configuration—the LC system known as the Multiple Use MARC System (MUMS) and that of OCLC, Inc. Because OCLC has more patrons nationwide than does the MUMS system, this type will be discussed in terms of the OCLC system. (More complete information about both the OCLC and MUMS authority systems is found in Chapter 5.)

In the OCLC system there exist two independent machine-readable files, a bibliographic file and an authority file. The bibliographic file consists of machine-readable bibliographic records from the LC MARC tapes, as well as MARC records contributed by the more than 2,000 contributing libraries that input records into the OCLC data base. There are established standards for the inputting of records and quality of information in the records, as well as a system of error reports and corrections. Members are supposed to consult the on-line authority file and to use the forms found there on records they add. Errors are tallied against libraries that violate this rule. The authority file, on the other hand, derives from one source only—it consists of LC authority records. There is no direct electronic link between records in the authority file and records in the bibliographic file. Both files have to be treated as two separate and independent data bases.

Authority File "Coordinated" with Bibliographic File

The second type of linkage arrangement I have chosen to call "coordination." The discussion of the card-based system assumed a coordinated arrangement. The authority file and bibliographic file are physically separate, but the authorized forms of names used in the bibliographic file are recorded in the authority file. When a change is made in the authority file, however, it is not always transmitted immediately to the bibliographic file. This time lag occurs because the name changed on one card in the authority file may appear on several bibliographic records. The process of maintenance of the catalog and the changing of catalog cards, or forms in the book or computer output microform (COM) catalog, does not occur rapidly.

Authority File as Part of Bibliographic File

Some libraries have chosen not to have a separate authority file, but instead to have their authorized forms of heading occur in the bibliographic file alone. Cross-references are made part of the catalog in various ways. Authority records as such do not exist, but the bibliographic file (sometimes called the official catalog) functions as an authority file, among other things. When changes of name occur, the appropriate section of the entire file is changed along with the cross-reference apparatus.

Cross-references are incorporated into the bibliographic file in three ways:

1. only cross-references and history cards are used;

2. cross-references are placed on the bibliographic record itself (the forms referred from are usually typed on the back of the main entry of the bibliographic record that first uses that name);

3. a combination of 1 and 2.

In these ways, the syndetic structure of the catalog still exists, although in a less than desirable state. The card bearing the cross-reference data, for example, can be removed or altered without a corresponding change in the cards bearing the *see from* and *see also from* references.

Authority File in Direct Electronic Connection with Bibliographic File

Perhaps the ideal situation is the direct electronic linkage of the authority file with the bibliographic file. Such systems as the Washington Library Network (WLN) and the University of California's MELVYL use such a link. In outline, they work like this: There are two distinct files, the authority file and the bibliographic file. When a heading in the authority file is used in the bibliographic file, a pointer, or electronic link, is made from the authority record in the authority file to all appropriate records in the bibliographic file. The heading is stored only once, in the authority file. In addition, the bibliographic file contains pointers from it to the heading in the authority file. When the authority file record is changed, therefore, only the authority record need be changed. The pointers to the bibliographic record remain intact, and this obviates the need for changing the headings in the bibliographic file.

CHANGES IN AUTHORITY DATA

Discovery of Needed Changes

Needed changes in authority data can be discovered in a number of ways. Most commonly the discovery is made during cataloging, during acquisition, and during the use of the catalog by reference personnel or patrons.

When a cataloger catalogs a book and discovers that a name chosen as an access point is already in the authority file, the name is usually checked against the new evidence in the material cataloged in order to see if any changes are needed in the authority record; if the name established is still valid in view of the new evidence; if any new cross-references must be made; or if any other information needs to be added to the authority record, such as notes, death dates, or the like. In similar ways, acquisitions personnel and, less frequently, users and reference personnel, may discover what appear to be anomalies in authority data or in headings used in bibliographic records. When these are discovered, they are usually referred to catalogers or others primarily responsible for authority work, for evaluation and possible inclusion in affected authority records.

Evaluation of Whether Changes Are Needed

It goes without saying that if a cataloger discovers an error in the authority file in the process of cataloging or determines that a change in an authority record is needed, the cataloger makes the necessary changes. What happens, however, if one of the other persons mentioned above thinks that a change in the heading or authority file is necessary? The action taken depends in large part on the policy in effect within the library. There should be some type of procedural guide not only for making changes, but also for referring possible changes to those in charge of making them. In evaluating whether a change should be made, the cataloger essentially goes through the same process as when the heading was formed initially. The cataloging code in effect, the RIs that are currently active, and local practice rules are all consulted to see if the name or title in the present authority record is still correct. Cross-references are also judged in a similar manner. If changes are to be made, a procedural guide is a must.

How Changes Are Carried Out

The changing of a record in the authority file requires more than the knowledge of how to erase and/or replace a heading in a data base. It also requires a complete knowledge of the rules and RIs that affect those rules. Further, it requires a knowledge of the entire system involved and the various files, records, and catalog users that the particular change will affect. The process can become most confusing at the level of system knowledge, much to the surprise of the novice cataloger who looks upon application of cataloging rules as an exercise in transcendental logic. That is why a procedural guide is an absolute necessity. Without it, the changer of authority data can be left bewildered, and the effect of the change, even though it may be correct, will not be felt where it should be. Furthermore, the changing of authority records is a labor-intensive activity. In card-based systems it may involve noting that the change is required, checking the rules to ensure that it is required, and pulling the old authority record from the authority file, together with its cross-reference cards. Then a new authority record set must be typed up, and finally the change must be made in the bibliographic file. Depending on the guidelines for making necessary changes, this can affect one, some, or numerous records. With extremely stringent rules about the punctuation and appearance of authority records, a great number of authority cards may have to be changed. With less stringent rules about these matters, and rules that concentrate on "substantive" changes, the number of changes required could be considerably less. In automated systems, the time involved in changing authority records is much shorter than in card-based systems, but the activity itself is still labor intensive and is despised by many catalogers, who prefer to produce new catalog records.

The OCLC Conversion: Massive Changes in a Computerized Data Base

One of the most massive and interesting changes in a computerized data base in recent years was the OCLC "flip," in which many records in the OCLC bibliographic file were changed to conform to LC authority records. The OCLC system, you will recall, consists of two independent files, the authority file and the bibliographic file. In this arrangement lay the problem.

In January 1981 the Library of Congress planned to adopt the second edition of the *Anglo-American Cataloguing Rules,* which was published in 1978. Since the first day of publication, AACR2 had been the focus of controversy. Arguments flew back and forth in the library press concerning the infeasibility of one rule or another, the difficulties of changing catalogs from one set of rules to another, and so on. (It was rarely mentioned that any catalogs in existence since 1900 had already suffered five changes of rules and were, in fact, an amalgam of five different codes.)

At OCLC, the administration faced a formidable task. How would the headings in the data base be converted from earlier forms to AACR2 forms of names? It was clearly impossible to reevaluate each heading individually to comply with the new rules. The decision was made to use any available AACR2 headings sanctioned by the Library of Congress and to ensure that those headings were converted in the data base. The sources of the sanctioned headings were the LC name authority tapes that OCLC received on a regular basis from the Library of Congress. Since the publication of AACR2 in 1978, the Library of Congress had been gathering AACR2 forms for records during its own cataloging process. When a form required by the new rules did not already exist in the machine-readable authority file, the library created one. It then distributed these AACR2 and AACR2-compatible[4] headings on its weekly shipment of authority records. Since AACR2 was not yet official, however, the Library of Congress could not issue these new headings as valid headings, but only as cross-references, with a code signifying that the heading was AACR2.

OCLC had been receiving these tapes for some time and had been integrating them with its on-line authority file. If the data base of bibliographic records was to receive these new AACR2 headings, a very complicated and time-consuming process would have to be followed. First, any AACR2 heading in an authority record would have to be reassigned from its cross-reference status to an authorized heading status. The former heading would be transferred to a cross-reference status. Then, once this was accomplished, the authority file would have to be matched against the headings of the bibliographic file. When a match occurred with a cross-reference or an authorized heading, the actual AACR2 heading would be transferred to occupy the position of authorized heading in the bibliographic record. The former heading in the bibliographic record would be placed in yet another field (87x) within the bibliographic record. Finally, an indication on the bibliographic record would be made that specific headings were now in AACR2 form (through the use of the $w subfield).

OCLC essentially closed down its data base for two weeks in December 1980. The process described above took place during that time.[5]

From January 1981 onward, OCLC members were asked to indicate the status of the heading on the records that they added to the data base, using a special code in a subfield ($w) of each heading. The first part of the two-character code referred to the author part of the heading, the second to the title part. If either part was absent, the letter n was used. The codes had the following meanings:

1—AACR2 form verified on-line by user

3—AACR2 form supplied by user. Cataloging copy in hand; piece not in hand

4—AACR2 form supplied by user. Cataloging copy and piece in hand

m—AACR2 form constructed by OCLC system manipulation of text

n—unaffected or not applicable

c—AACR2 form transferred from LC name authority file by OCLC system

d—AACR2-compatible form transferred from LC name authority file by OCLC system[6]

The consequences of the flip revealed two things to library system users. First of all, the hitherto theoretical advantages of a linked file with the authorized heading stored only once were made palpably clear. Second, even the best designed algorithm for matching and manipulating authority or bibliographic data fell short of expectations. This lesson had been learned by computer personnel in the past. Such knowledge was now embarrassingly familiar to librarians as well.

NOTES

1.   Helen Schmierer labels these steps "verification" and "using established forms as access points." See her "The Relationship of Authority Control to the Library Catalog," *Illinois Libraries* 65:599-603 (September 1980).

2.   Betsy Baker and Kathleen Kluegel, "Availability and Use of OCLC for Reference in a Large Academic Library," *RQ* 21:379-383 (Summer 1982).

3.   For further discussion of types of links see Robert H. Burger, "Artificial Intelligence and Authority Control," *Library Resources and Technical Services* 28(4):337-345 (October/December 1984).

4.   An LC-compatible heading is, in fact, another form of superimposition—the policy of adopting a new catalog code while leaving headings derived from an earlier code unrevised. It is cleverly defined by LC in *Cataloging Service Bulletin* (6):6 (Fall 1979) thus: "In assessing AACR2, the Library has identified several categories for which needed changes, although desirable, do not significantly affect the filing arrangement and consequently the user's access. Therefore, LC, in general, plans to continue to use such headings that already exist."

5.   Arnold Wajenberg and Michael Gorman, "The OCLC Data Base Conversion: A User's Perspective," *Journal of Library Automation* 14(3):174-189 (September 1981).

6.   *Bibliographic Input Standards,* 2d ed. (Dublin, Ohio: OCLC, 1982), Intro:12-Intro:13.

4

THE MEASUREMENT AND EVALUATION OF AUTHORITY SYSTEMS

Library managers evaluate information retrieval systems in order to make decisions about them. The specific types of evaluation undertaken, as well as the decisions made, differ from one type of system to another. As we saw in Chapter 1, the model of an authority system includes several components. Administrative decisions must be made from time to time about the individual components; these decisions, in turn, may or may not affect other components in the system. Furthermore, these decisions must be made (1) in order to avoid, or at least reduce, the incidence of system failures and (2) with economic considerations in mind. Intelligent decisions, however, cannot be made about any aspect of the system without adequate descriptive information about the components of the system and a means for determining whether the system is carrying out the goals set for it. This chapter will cover some basic measurements necessary to describe an authority system, as well as methods that could be and are used to determine whether it is achieving its goals.

To some it may seem unnecessary to deal with the measurement and evaluation of an authority system. After all, authority systems can be considered part of library catalogs, which are specialized information retrieval systems. Evaluation is conducted for the whole system, not exclusively for one part.

Such a viewpoint, however, is shortsighted. Authority control accomplishes the finding and gathering functions of the catalog. When the entire catalog is evaluated, its functions must be considered, and this consideration leads directly back to authority control. Evaluation of the catalog cannot be carried out without the systematic evaluation of authority control.

STEPS IN EVALUATION

There are two steps in evaluation: description and comparison. King and Bryant have written:

> We *describe* systems in order to acquire knowledge of their operating characteristics under specific environmental conditions, and we *compare* alternative systems with regard to particular characteristics. Both description and comparison require specification of system characteristics, or measurement.[1]

When we describe authority systems we can discuss both functional and quantitative characteristics. Both enable us to be specific about what we are describing. Chapters 2 and 3 indicated the functional characteristics of authority records and files, their components, and the purposes they serve. We could also quantify some of these characteristics by measuring the length of each authority record in bytes, or the average number of cross-references per authority record, or the number of records existing in any system at a given time. Depending on the type of system used, card- or machine-based, we may want to know these and other quantitative characteristics in order to satisfy managerial requests for information so that intelligent decisions may be made.

For several years now, for example, Williams, Barth, and Preece have provided statistics on MARC *bibliographic* records in order to build up a statistical data base of measurable features of bibliographic records and their components.[2] The gathering of this data is indispensable to the design and implementation of automated library catalogs. No such studies have been reported for machine-readable authority data. In fact, I have not found any evidence of comprehensive evaluation of authority systems at all. What now passes for evaluation is an elaborate system of quality control. That is, authority records are subject to rigorous review *prior* to their filing or entrance into the card or machine-readable authority file.

As we shall see later in this chapter, most evaluative activity now focuses on only one of the three main areas of evaluation—questions relating to the preparation of authority data. This type of evaluation deals with five areas: legality of data, legality of format, accuracy of data, accuracy of format, and comprehensiveness of data. Let us discuss each of these in turn.

Legality of Data

In any authority system, the most important aspect of the data it contains is its legality—i.e., conformity with cataloging codes, LC RIs, and local practice. There are two ways of evaluating systems according to these criteria. The data may be evaluated as they enter the system or, once in the system, they may be sampled to determine probable errors. A respected library philosopher who wishes to remain anonymous once remarked, "The library is a place of mistakes." He was not, I assure you, referring to the people working in libraries, but meant rather that because there are so many opportunities for making mistakes, mistakes will happen.

This is common knowledge in libraries, and as a result technical services personnel have set up elaborate systems for checking and revising cataloging and authority data prior to their entry into the system. Such procedures may consist of one cataloger revising the work of other catalogers, catalogers exchanging work and revising each other's work, the funneling of work or copy slips and authority cards to a centralized location for review by a quality control team, or various combinations of these methods. This checking practice usually includes checking the cataloging or authority data to see that they conform with AACR2, LC RIs, and local policy. The problem with such revising and checking is knowing the extent to which it should be done. One way of deciding who gets evaluated or to what extent is to devise some sort of point system for errors, to revise progressively fewer copy slips or authority cards as a cataloger becomes more experienced, or to exclude certain categories of cataloging from review on the assumption that they have already been reviewed by a competent authority (e.g., LC catalog cards or authority data). The other way of assuring the legality of data is by sampling the authority file after it has been made and thoroughly checking those sampled items for errors. If the error rate is unacceptably high, a process may have to be instituted to check the records before they enter the file.

Of course, the safest way of assuring quality data is by checking the records before they become part of the file. It is usually more difficult, although considerably less expensive, to identify errors once the file is formed than it is to identify them before the file is formed.

Legality of Format

The format of an authority file is the "envelope" into which the data is placed to communicate it to others within a system. For card-based systems this usually consists of instructions prescribing the placement of the various elements of authority data on the authority card. In machine-based systems, this entails the correct coding of the authority record.[3]   In both systems, format is necessary to avoid ambiguity and give consistency to the information recorded. Legality of format, then, refers to the adherence to the prescription for formatting of the authority data. Headings in a machine-based system, for example, must be coded in the 1xx fields, not the 4xx or 260 fields. In card-based systems, cross-references must be preceded by a lowercase x to indicate *see from* references and by two lowercase xx's to indicate *see also from* references. If the prescribed format for the data recorded is not used, authority systems will not function. Legality of data and format are closely related to accuracy of data and format.

Accuracy of Data

Accuracy of data is related to legality of data, but it is different enough to warrant separate discussion. The legality of data must always be checked by personnel who have the knowledge and experience to spot a "legal" error. Such people must be highly familiar with the cataloging codes and other prescriptive rules for authority data. But the accuracy of data does not have to be checked by highly trained and experienced personnel. In the case of coding machine-readable records, many errors are caught by editing programs that can identify the more egregious coding mistakes. Misspellings of names and other typographical errors can be handled by technical assistants or clerical personnel. However, in many cases the highly trained person catches both kinds of errors.

Accuracy of Format

In many systems, those who check card-based authorities check for accuracy and legality at the same time. In machine-based systems, however, the work can be divided between person and machine—the human reviewer checks for legality of data, and the machine can be programmed to check for accuracy of format. The legality of format cannot be checked by the machine. A program can check against a table to see if each tag and subfield code encountered is allowed and if mandatory fields, codes, and combinations are present, but it would be impossible for a machine to determine if the data contained within a given field were properly coded.

Comprehensiveness of Data

In many cases, cross-references and notes are added to authority records both to provide a cross-reference structure for the catalog and to provide information to users of the authority file, so that they may make appropriate decisions with regard to searching and construction of related authority records. The determination of whether the information on an authority record is comprehensive enough and whether it includes sufficient cross-references and notes about the heading can usually only be based on experience. Although guidelines are provided by AACR2 and by local cataloging policy, experience both in cataloging and in public service is invaluable. The public service component is important because catalogers, like most people, tend to view the world solely from their own perspective. By working with the public in libraries, catalogers can observe how others use the products of cataloging and thereby see new implications for their decisions once they are back at the cataloging desk. With this experience specific kinds of references may become more important, such as from nonentry parts of compound surnames or variant forms of personal or corporate names found in different sources.

OTHER TYPES OF EVALUATION

The types of evaluation discussed above are not enough. If intelligent decisions are to be made about the management of authority files, other facts must be known. Little work has been done in the area of evaluating name authority systems; this crucial task can be broken down into at least three components:

1. questions related to the preparation of authority records

2. questions related to the description of completed authority records

3. questions related to the behavior of authority records and files under different environmental conditions

These three components can be further broken down into the lists of questions that follow.

Preparation of Authority Records

1. Are the rules and rule interpretations followed consistently by all catalogers?

2. Do all catalogers have the necessary documentation, or access to it, that will ensure consistency with other catalogers?

3. Are the rules and rule interpretations well written? Are the rules clear and free of ambiguity?

4. Do revisers of authority records perform consistently and according to some measurable standard?

5. What is the length of time required to prepare an authority record?

6. What are the tasks in a given library necessary to prepare an authority record?

7. Are authority records prepared for all entries?

8. How extensively does the cataloger search to validate the form of name chosen for an entry?

9. Are authority records entered quickly into the system so that duplicate records are not created?

10. Is a clear record kept of changes in the policy for preparation of authority records?

Description of Completed Authority Records

1. What is the frequency of such authority record elements as *see from* references, *see also from* references, notes, citations of evidence necessary to establish the heading, etc.?

2. For machine-readable authority records, what is the length, in bytes, of the authority records?

3. For machine-readable authority records, what is the average length of the various fields in an authority record?

Behavior of Authority Records and Files under Different Environmental Conditions

1. Does the authority system accomplish the finding and gathering functions?

2. Does the authority system penalize the searcher for using variant (non-authoritative) forms of names?

3. Do variant forms of names lead directly to bibliographic records, through the mechanism of the catalog (delegated search), or indirectly to bibliographic records, by requiring the entry of the authorized form (augmented search)?[4]

4. Are the authority displays and system messages simple enough to be understood by the average patron?

5. Is enough information given in the displays?

6. How quickly is the authority file growing?

7. What is the number of changes in a specific time period that must be made to the existing authority file?

8. What are the space requirements for the authority file?

By answering these sets of questions, the administrator can begin to understand the unique system he or she is dealing with. All the questions warrant further discussion, but I would like to focus on the problem of file growth and change (items 6 and 7) of the last set of questions) in order to show how answers to earlier questions are necessary to answer these two.

Measurement of the Rate of Growth of Authority Files

Authority files are bibliometrically related to bibliographic files, and bibliographic files are related to knowledge as a whole. Many measurements have been made of the growth of knowledge. This is a lively topic that has its share of controversy. Several laws governing the growth of knowledge and the growth of literature have been formulated, among them Zipf's law, Bradford's law, and Lotka's law.[5] Various measurements of obsolescence and scattering in literatures have also been made. These laws have been shown to apply to the literature of various fields, and evidence exists that Lotka's law at least has some application to specific library catalogs.[6] But here's the rub—bibliometrics has not been applied at all to authority files, and rarely to library catalogs. Authority files and their rate of growth and change have chiefly been the concern of librarians, for such files, by and large, do not exist outside the library world, although they are present in some nonlibrary information retrieval systems. The other complicating factor is that many of the bibliometric laws now discovered, and especially Lotka's law, which relates authors and number of publications, have been formulated on the basis of journal literature, and not books, records, scores, maps, and other published material. They also deal only with personal authors, and not other types of access points. So the first issue that must be analyzed is the relationship of growth of authority files to existing laws of bibliometrics and the factors that influence the growth of authority files.

Authority File Growth in Outline: The Central Factors

If we assume that when we are talking about the growth of an authority file, we are talking about a file based upon a specific collection, then we may postulate that the number of authority records is directly dependent on the number of bibliographic records in that collection. Whenever authority records are made as a result of the cataloging process, this assumption must hold.

We know from Lotka's law that the number of authors that produce more than one publication decreases in relation to the number of publications issued. In Lotka's formulation, "the number [of authors] making n contributions is about $1/n^2$ of those making one; and the proportion of all contributors, that make a single contribution, is about 60 percent."[7] From this we may assume that authority files will grow very fast initially, since there is only a small probability that an author being entered into the file will have a record there already. Past a certain point, however, when x number of records have accumulated, this rate of increase will slow down and will depend more on other factors, as yet unknown. The other problem, however, is that we can examine an authority file synchronically, but we wish to know information about it diachronically. In other words, we can learn facts about an authority file at a given point, but we wish to know about its behavior over a specific span of time.

Another major factor affecting the growth of authority files is that individual authors are not the only names for which authority records exist. Even if we leave aside the question of subject authorities (as is done in this book), we must be able to make some type of determination of the number of other created headings, such as corporate bodies, uniform titles, geographic names, conference names, and series in relation to bibliographic records in general. Furthermore, whether such headings are created is dependent on the cataloging rules in effect at the time, local policy with regard to tracing, and the quality control of cataloging and authority work. On the basis of the foregoing discussion all we can state at present is the following:

The growth of authority files in a particular library is dependent on a number of factors:

1. the growth (G) of the bibliographic file

2. the type (T) of bibliographic file (specific or general)[8]

3. the cataloging rules (R) in effect

4. other local or national policies (P), relating to tracings or headings

5. the frequency of other not previously traced nonauthor headings per bibliographic record (H/B)

We can depict the growth of the authority file (G_a) as a function (f) of these factors, thus:

$$G_a = f(G, T, R, P, H/B)$$

Furthermore, we know that:

1. authority files grow very fast initially, but slow down once the file has reached a maturity of some sort;

2. once authority files reach maturity, their growth can be affected by changes in collection priorities and cataloging priorities.

Changes in Authority Data

The other problem mentioned above is the rate of change of authority data. Librarians in catalog/authority file maintenance need data relating to changes in authority data in order to estimate staffing and equipment needs. As we saw in Chapter 3, changes can come about from several sources and may be of various types. They may include, but are certainly not limited to:

1. simple typographic errors (E)

2. changes as a result of cataloging rules (R)

3. changes as a result of local or national policy (P)

4. tolerance limits (L) for mistakes and effects on retrieval

Mathematically, we can express this as:

$$\text{Rate of change} = f(E, R, P, L)$$

Studies of individual catalogs are needed to test these hypothetical statements dealing with growth and change.

System Failure and Economic Efficiency

Evaluation of authority systems can be undertaken from two other perspectives, system failure and economic efficiency. Often a system failure, once it is discovered, can be corrected by altering elements of the system. Some common system failures are:

1. a name chosen by the user is not an access point on the desired document ("user error")

2. a name chosen by the user was not chosen by the cataloger as a valid access point (system failure)

3. a variant form of name chosen by the user is not a valid cross-reference (system error)[9]

4. a valid form of name chosen by a user is incorrect in the system (possible clerical error)

5. the cross-reference structure does not work within the authority file

6. the cross-reference structure of the authority file is not mirrored accurately in the bibliographic file

7. changes made in the authority file are not made in the bibliographic file

In all of these cases, some action should be taken by the alert administrator, provided, of course, that such failures are observed and recorded and that they form some sort of pattern, suggesting that an alteration in procedures will eliminate the error. For example, if the type of failure in item 4 occurs often, increased review of authority records for accuracy might be considered. If the type of failure described in item 2 occurs, a reconsideration of adherence to national policy with regard to choice of access points may be in order.

Besides all this diagnostic work and all the suggestions to change this or that aspect of the system or to increase quality control, there is the other question of economic efficiency, asked earlier. That is, is the cost of following a particular policy worth the benefit gained as a result? The amount of information displayed, for example, may be more than users need. If this can be ascertained, it may be more efficient and cost beneficial to reduce the amount of authority information displayed to the user. On the other hand, accurate name authorities are vitally important. Therefore, extensive quality control during processing of authority records may be preferable to random sampling of the file at a later date in order to find errors in accuracy.

It should be clear from the foregoing discussion that while some evaluative work is currently carried out on authority systems, much more needs to be done. We need to develop a sense of the need for evaluation beyond quality control on data being entered; we need to develop techniques to answer the questions posed earlier in this chapter; and we need to gain expertise in applying the knowledge gained from these studies and bibliometrics to improve authority systems and the catalog as a whole.

NOTES

1.   Donald King and Edward C. Bryant, *Evaluation of Information Services and Products.* (Arlington, Va.: Information Resources Press, 1971), 7.

2.   Martha Williams, Stephen W. Barth, and Scott E. Preece, "Summary Statistics for Five Years of the MARC Data Base," *Journal of Library Automation* 12(4):314-337 (December 1979); see also Sally H. McCallum, "Statistics on Headings in the MARC File," *Journal of Library Automation* 14(3):194-201 (September 1981).

3.   For a discussion of the coding problems see Robert H. Burger, "Data Definition and the Decline of Cataloging Quality," *Library Journal* 108(18):1924-1926 (October 15, 1983).

4.   For a discussion of delegated vs. augmented searches, see Linda C. Smith, "Machine Intelligence vs. Machine-Aided Intelligence in Information Retrieval: A Historical Perspective," in *Research and Development in Information Retrieval: Proceedings,* Lecture Notes in Computer Science 146, ed. Gerard Salton and Hans-Jochen Schneider (Berlin and New York: Springer-Verlag, 1983), 263.

5.   For a definitive and enlightened discussion of these laws, see *Library Trends* 30(1) (Summer 1981), special issue on Bibliometrics, William C. Potter, ed.

6.   William G. Potter, "When Names Collide: Conflict in the Catalog and AACR2," *Library Resources and Technical Services* 24:3-16 (Winter 1980).

7.   Ibid. See also William G. Potter, "Lotka's Law Revisited," *Library Trends* 30(1) (Summer 1981), special issue on Bibliometrics, 7.

8.   A collection restricted in scope and type of material will probably conform more closely to Lotka's Law behavior than a general collection.

9.   Arlene G. Taylor, "Authority Files in Online Catalogs: An Investigation of Their Value," *Cataloging and Classification Quarterly* 4(3):1-17 (Spring 1984).

5

STATE-OF-THE-ART
AUTHORITY SYSTEMS

On-line public access catalogs (OPACs) have been compared from various points of view,[1] but none of the studies has focused sufficient attention on the authority control mechanism of the systems examined. Without such attention, understanding of the features common to these systems is inadequate, and comparisons of the systems are incomplete.

This chapter compares six automated authority systems (most of which are not accessible to the public) by classifying the chosen systems into three groups, specifying twenty-two characteristics by which such systems can be compared, and describing each system in terms of this set of characteristics. (Table 5.1, pp. 61-63, summarizes these descriptions.) The reader should understand that this study in no way attempts to compare all automated authority systems, nor even to compare the best or most advanced. It is first an exercise in determining the validity of the comparative approach in this context and second an attempt to assess whether major features of existing authority systems can be identified from existing source documentation.

Burger[2] has classified on-line authority systems into three categories: (1) those independent of the related bibliographic file; (2) those closely related to the bibliographic file but not electronically linked; and (3) those electronically linked to the bibliographic file. The systems to be examined in this chapter are categorized according to this system as follows: class 1–OCLC, Inc.; class 2–RLIN and Library of Congress; and class 3–New York Public Library, MELVYL, and WLN.

Obviously, the six systems chosen are not the only on-line authority systems, but they are the most widely used, or they exhibit features not found in other systems. In addition, the focus on these systems is more reliable and legitimate because of the existing published and unpublished literature about them. This literature, as well as personal communication with representatives of these systems, has served as the source documentation for this chapter.

It could be argued that class 1, in which the authority file is independent of the related bibliographic file, does not actually have anything to do with authority systems. Such an argument has some validity. If the purpose of an authority file is to record the form of names chosen as headings for a bibliographic file, as well as to record appropriate cross-references, source information, and other data relating to the chosen heading, then implicit in this definition is that the authority file and bibliographic file should be directly related.[3] In this class, however, they are not. The OCLC authority file, for example, consists of the LC MARC authority file, which is a read-only file. The only changes made to it are made by OCLC.

Member libraries do not have the capability or authority to alter it. The bibliographic file in OCLC consists of LC MARC bibliographic records, as well as member-contributed copy. There is no requirement that records contributed to the bibliographic file use the prescribed heading from the available authority file. The authority file is used only for reference. There is, of course, a relationship between the authority file (obtained from the Library of Congress) and the LC bibliographic records contained in OCLC, but this relationship is not as clear-cut as some would hope.[4]

In general terms, then, class 1 includes any system that has two separate files, an authority file and a bibliographic file, with no requirement that records in the bibliographic file contain the prescribed form of name from the authority file. The definition does not preclude a loose relationship between the two files.

Class 2 is a more desirable arrangement. Class 2 systems include authority and bibliographic files that are related to one another but are not electronically linked. That is, there is a requirement that names used as headings in bibliographic records must be those prescribed by the authority file or must be made part of the authority file when bibliographic records are added to the data base.

In class 3 systems, with an electronic linkage between authority file and bibliographic file, the bibliographic file sometimes does not contain headings at all, but only pointers in the computerized bibliographic record to related authority records that contain the prescribed form of name for that record. When the bibliographic record is displayed in such systems, the heading from the authority file is reassembled with the descriptive portion of the record and displayed to the user.

In order to distinguish between these three classes more clearly, let us assume that we have two editions of Mark Twain's *Huckleberry Finn,* one published in New York in 1920 and the other in Boston in 1935. Assume also that one library catalogs the 1920 edition and another library the 1935 edition. One decides to enter the record under Twain and the other under Clemens.

In a class 1 system, the records could appear as follows:

Authority Record	*Bibliographic Record*
Twain, Mark	Twain, Mark
xClemens, Samuel Langhorne	Adventures of Huckleberry Finn 1920
	Clemens, Samuel Langhorne
	Adventures of Huckleberry Finn 1935

Despite a valid authority record prescribing use of "Twain, Mark" as the authorized heading, the headings in the bibliographic records differ. One library has decided to enter the 1920 edition under Twain and the other has decided to enter the 1935 edition under Clemens. In spite of the authority file that prescribed Twain, the difference remains, and unless a search is made for both Twain and Clemens, these two books by the same author would probably not be retrieved.

In a class 2 system, the records could appear as follows:

Authority record	*Bibliographic record*
Twain, Mark	Twain, Mark
xClemens, Samuel Langhorne	Adventures of Huckleberry Finn 1920
	Twain, Mark
	Adventures of Huckleberry Finn 1935

The relationship between the authority file and the bibliographic file dictates that the prescribed form of name in the authority file be used for records in the bibliographic file. The prescribed form is used for both bibliographic records and both would be retrieved, but a search of the authority file might have to be made to confirm the proper form of name. Such a system, however, assures the user that different forms of name are resolved with the authority record and that records in the bibliographic file are entered only under the prescribed form (depending, of course, upon the intellectual link made by the person entering the record).

In a class 3 system, the records could appear as follows:

Authority Record	*Bibliographic Record*
(Record 2345)	(Authority Record 2345)
Twain, Mark	Adventures of Huckleberry Finn 1920
xClemens, Samuel Langhorne	
	(Authority Record 2345)
	Adventures of Huckleberry Finn 1935

In this class, different forms of name are resolved by the authority record, but the capability also exists to search only the authority file in order to retrieve items from the bibliographic file. In other words, there is only one index necessary for retrieval from both files.

Now that these systems have been classed, let us look in more detail not only at the characteristics of the individual systems that prompted such classification, but also at other salient characteristics that will be used to compare the six systems. The characteristics chosen for the comparison, along with their definitions, follow.

THE DATA BASE

1. *Data source.* Authority files can be built from a variety of sources, such as LC authority records (which themselves are made up of LC authority records and records contributed by NACO Project[5] member libraries), headings from bibliographic records, and locally produced and input authority records. Some systems use all three sources; others restrict themselves to one.

2. *Internal format.* Within any system the authority record is contained in some type of record format. Many systems receive the authority records in the MARC communications format, but they often house this information in a different format. This can be a record format or a data base management system such as the Adaptable Database System (ADABAS), the MARC record format itself, or some other locally produced vehicle. The type of internal format affects the system's ability to transfer authority data to other institutions and its ability to change the format when changes are made in other formats with which the institution deals.

3. *Capability for handling information from MARC records.* Some internal formats can handle all MARC fields; others filter out everything except the fields or information considered most important.

4. *Resolution of information from MARC tapes.* Even though an internal format may use all the information from a MARC authority tape, it may not provide sufficient resolution of this information for subsequent retrieval. All notes, for example, may be compressed into one giant note field. All cross-references may be compressed into a cross-reference field rather than individual fields for each cross-reference.

5. *Size of authority file vs. size of bibliographic file.* The relative size of an authority file with respect to its related data base can indicate the level of authority control achieved.[6]

DATA BASE PROCESSING

6. *Addition of new records.* Are new records added to the authority file automatically by program or by an input operator manually? Some systems provide for both types of addition for different kinds of records.

7. *Method of changing file.* The Cataloging Distribution Service provides changes to authority records on its weekly authority tapes. Can the system process these changes by program, or are they ignored or added manually?

8. *Manual editing.* Can maintenance personnel enter the file and change existing authority records?

9. *87x fields used to make cross-references.* Are 87x fields in the bibliographic file used to create cross-references in the authority record? The 87x field contains a cross-reference form of name and can be used in bibliographic records to provide a cross-reference form of name in that record. Some systems may have the capability to use these 87x fields to create cross-references to the established form of heading.

QUALITY CONTROL

10. *Error correction devices for format.* If the system uses bibliographic records and/or other authority records for its data source, does it include the capability to check for format errors in the incoming information?

11. *Error correction devices for content.* Does the system include any way of detecting errors in content, e.g., missing fields?

12. *Review of new headings.* Are new headings, either on a printout or in a work file in the computer, reviewed by qualified personnel?

13. *Level of development of maintenance routines.* One facet of on-line systems that always seems to be ignored or given short shrift is maintenance. When several data sources are used and there are various ways of correcting certain errors, there must be some guidelines for determining the preferred method and order of correcting errors.

14. *Security.* Is there a system to prevent unauthorized access to the authority file or unauthorized maintenance of it?

PUBLIC DISPLAY/USE

15. *Types of display formats.* Some systems have several types of display formats, depending on the type of information needed. What are these and what is their purpose?

16. *Searching of file.* What elements are used; what form can they take (truncated or full), and how are they linked (e.g., Boolean logic or concatenation in a search key)?

17. *Authorized form displayed on retrieval.* Is there a need to rekey the authorized form of name when it is found or does the search automatically link the authority record to the related bibliographic records?

18. *Links to circulation system.* Are there links to the circulation system and reverse?

19. *Links to other files.* Are there links to other files in the system?

EVALUATION

20. *Descriptive information available.* Are descriptive statistics compiled on use, or are logs of failed searches kept?

21. *User feedback.* Is there any method of feedback from the users for the authority file (questionnaires, surveys, etc.)?

22. *Other evaluative procedures.* Since this is a relatively infant field, there may or may not be any information gathered here.

DESCRIPTION OF INDIVIDUAL SYSTEMS

Class 1

OCLC, Inc.

OCLC, located in Dublin, Ohio, presently has more bibliographic records in its files (more than 11,500,000) than any other bibliographic utility. It services more than 2,000 libraries both in the United States and abroad. The size of the authority file is approximately 1,000,000 records.

The Data Base

The OCLC authority file consists of machine-readable authority records purchased from the Library of Congress. It does not contain subject authority records. Member libraries do not contribute authority data directly to OCLC. Libraries participating in the NACO Project, some of whom are members of OCLC, do construct authority records; however, these records are not input on-line like bibliographic records, but are sent directly to the Library of Congress for authentication and distribution. The authority file uses the MARC format, with some additional information provided by OCLC.[7] The ratio of authority records to bibliographic records is approximately 1:11.[8]

Data Base Processing

New records are added to the file as they are received from the Library of Congress, and changed records are processed. There is no manual editing, and 87x fields are not used to create new headings.

Quality Control

Error detection programs ensure that each new record conforms to the prescribed organization, such as tag and subject combinations. There is no human review of new headings, and no maintenance routines are connected with the authority file. The major security device is that it is a read-only file for OCLC users.

Public Display/Use

The slightly modified MARC format is used for display. The search key used is the same 4, 3, 1 or 3, 2, 2, 1 search key used for all types of names and uniform titles and series. There is no link to the bibliographic file, although there may appear to be to a naive user. Such a misconception may come about in the following way. If a user has retrieved a specific bibliographic record and then enters a search key from an entry of that bibliographic record (or any reasonable search key), name authority records that match that key will be retrieved. It is then possible to return to previous displays in the bibliographic retrieval sequence and in the name authority retrieval sequence by using commands designed for retrieval of previous displays. This does not mean, however, that the name authority records and the bibliographic records are linked within the system. The terminal buffer simply stores the displays previously retrieved in one sequence each for authority records and for bibliographic records (as many as nine screens) and redisplays on command.[9]

Evaluation

No evaluation is attempted. Users may comment on the inaccuracy of authority data, but these comments are referred to the Library of Congress for action.

Class 2

Research Libraries Information Network (RLIN)[10]

The Data Base

The RLIN authority file consists of LC MARC authority records (names only) and New York Public Library (NYPL) authority records (names and subjects). Both sets of records are in the MARC format and have full resolution. As of July 1984 the size of the authority file is numbered 2.345 million records. There is some overlap between the LC and NYPL files. The ratio of authority file to bibliographic file is approximately 1:6. The bibliographic file of 12.7 million records also includes duplicate records. This bibliographic file is not a master record file (i.e., for each authorized heading there is no one "master" record to which all others are subordinate.)

Data Base Processing

The file is updated regularly in batch mode using LC MARC authority tapes. No manual editing capability is currently available. The 87x fields are not used for cross-references, since bibliographic records are not used to form the file.

Quality Control

An error detection program checks for valid content designators. New headings are not manually reviewed, and automated maintenance routines are nonexistent. The file is read-only and is therefore secure.

Public Display/Use

The file is searchable by RLIN users or by anyone with an RLIN search-only account. Until early 1985, the display format will have been equivalent to the MARC authority format. After that, Research Libraries Group of Stanford, Calif., will have implemented a variety of display formats. There is no electronic link to any file.

Evaluation

Descriptive statistics regarding search strategies used and system resources consumed are provided by the system. There is no organized feedback from users. No other evaluation procedures are used.

Library of Congress[11]

The Data Base

The Library of Congress authority file consists exclusively of records produced by LC catalogers and authorized NACO Project participants. The records are currently produced on a work form that uses MARC tagging, but the internal LC displays are mnemonic. Naturally, the formats have complete MARC handling capability and full resolution. The size of the current file is approximately 1,000,000 records. The ratio of authority to bibliographic records is 2:5.

Data Base Processing

New records are added daily to the authority file. First, early notice records (ENRs) that contain the heading and some source information, but no cross-references, are input to the file on the day the authority record is approved. These ENRs are available for perusal by LC catalogers. Once the Library completes the manual processing of the full authority record, the remaining elements of it are input, using the ENR as a base record. New records are added at the rate of about 2,000 cards per week. Catalogers and other personnel involved with the cataloging process can change the file by submitting a change request that is processed manually through a terminal. The 87x fields are not used to create cross-references, since the bibliographic and authority files are not linked.

Quality Control

There is extremely strict adherence to the rules for constructing authority records as well as the rules in AACR2 and the Library of Congress rule interpretations. Error checks are made before the record is admitted to the file, and new headings are reviewed prior to their inputting into the file. The maintenance routines are highly developed and often complicated. Security is tight, as the file is, for all intents and purposes, a read-only file. Changes are initiated by catalogers. Changes to the data base itself, however, are entrusted only to personnel in the MARC editorial division.

Public Display/Use

Two types of internal formats are used: the PCRD and NCRD display. (NCRD includes full content designation; PCRD does not.) These displays give information in addition to that provided by the MARC fields for processing at the Library of Congress itself. Searching is done by specifying the type of name to be searched. Truncation, as well as full forms of names, is used in a Boolean type of retrieval. Once retrieved, the authorized form does appear on the screen. There is no electronic link to the bibliographic file.

Evaluation

Descriptive statistics are provided by the system. Users often submit inquiries about apparent errors in the authority file. No other evaluative procedures are available.

Class 3

New York Public Library[1][2]

The New York Public 'Library computer system, in existence since 1972, has undergone various changes and has added several improvements. The authority segment of this system is part of ONLICATS (*ONLI*ne *CAT*aloging *S*ystem). ONLICATS supports maintenance of both bibliographic and authority files.

The Data Base

Authority records are created from two sources: originally input bibliographic records and MARC bibliographic records. The headings from these records are used to formulate the system authority records. The authorized headings can then be augmented with notes and cross-references to form authority records. The notes and cross-references are added through manual input. The authority record uses MARC tagging, and hence is MARC compatible, but it does not include all authorized fields. The internal format is locally designed. The ratio of authority file to bibliographic file is 1:2, (approximately 1,000,000 authority records to 2,000,000 bibliographic records). This ratio is misleading, however. The figures are based on two separate data bases, each with its own authority file. One, the NYPL data base, has 520,792 authority records and 231,560 bibliographic records (ratio: 2:1). The other, MILCS (Metropolitan Interlibrary Cooperative System) has 647,569 authority records and 2,000,000 bibliographic records, 1,000,000 of which are not under authority control.

Data Base Processing

New records are only added as a result of cataloging. LC authority tapes are not used to add or change records. The existing authority file can be changed manually only by personnel in the Network Validation Center. There is no use of 87x fields for the creation of cross-references.

Quality Control

The maintenance and editing of the file is accomplished in either batch mode or one record at a time, for the most part immediately following input of a bibliographic record from which the authority record is made. In the on-line mode, the authority record to be edited is displayed on the screen and may be augmented, changed, or deleted. This updated copy of the record is then submitted to the system's edit checks, which validate the tags, indicators, and subfield codes of the record. After successfully passing this check, the record is replaced in the file in an "accept status." Since only one error is caught at a time and displayed, each record could conceivably be submitted more than once to the editing systems. Once this is accomplished, the bibliographic record is linked to the proper authority records in the system. Rigorous control is exercised over this linkage. According to the NYPL manual (p. IV-6), it cannot be broken except:

"(1)   When the bibliographic field is either deleted or changed, or the entire bibliographic record is deleted from the file; or

(2)   the linkage is specifically transferred to another authority record" through use of a specific system command.

Public Display/Use

Several types of display formats are available. The display received in response to a search is determined by parameters entered when the specific terminal is signed on. Search keys can be used with truncation. The authorized form is displayed on retrieval. There is no link to the circulation system, only to the bibliographic file.

Evaluation

Rigorous control is exercised over the entry of records into the system. There seems to be no other evaluative activity connected with the authority file once it is formed.

MELVYL[13]

The Data Base

MELVYL is the University of California On-Line Union Catalog. It contains records from all nine University of California campuses and is used by people at each of those nine campuses. The system operated in a prototype mode for about one year. In the spring of 1983 it went into production mode. As of June 28, 1984, it contained approximately 1,176,287 bibliographic records (representing more than 3.5 million holdings) and 2.2 million authority records (including subjects). The LC name authority machine-readable file is the only source used for full authority information. Since the LC file did not contain series until recently, there was no attempt to control these access points when the system was designed. Such control is anticipated in the future. The system also uses data extracted from "incoming" bibliographic records. It uses ADABAS as its data base management system and therefore internally has an ADABAS format that contains full MARC handling capability. The ratio of authority to bibliographic records is approximately 2:1, a high ratio due to a large, undetermined number of duplicate records.

Data Base Processing

At present the authority file is relatively static. Update tapes are not currently used to add to the file or to change it. Although manual editing capability is planned, there is now no method of changing authority records once they are in the file. The 87x fields are not used to create cross-references, although this feature is contemplated.

Quality Control

A well-developed error detection system checks for legality of tags, indicators, and subfields. The same programs also check for the presence of specific tags (e.g., 008 field). New headings are not reviewed. The file is read only and therefore secure.

Public Display/Use

There is no public display of the authority file, or, to put it more accurately, the availability of such a display is not advertised. The display includes labels such as Heading, See From, etc.

The new edition of the authority format is not used at present, but MELVYL plans to use it once the appropriate software is written.

Search key specificity is high. The use of Boolean operators is possible, and truncation is available for use with corporate names. Since this is a union file, there is no link to other systems, such as circulation.

Evaluation

Evaluation of the existing system takes place in two ways: through transaction analyses and questionnaires. Although search strategies and general patterns of search failure are revealed by such methods, there seems to be no independent evaluation of the authority file itself. New programs are being written to give expanded transaction analysis for the production data base.

Washington Library Network (WLN)[14]

The WLN computer system is a multipurpose bibliographic utility that provides many services such as bibliographic data base searching, cooperative cataloging, acquisition services, and product generation (catalog cards, labels, on-demand bibliographies, etc.). The system was implemented in 1977. The authority system is part of the bibliographic subsystem.

The Data Base

Authority data comes from two sources: headings from bibliographic records input into the system, and authority records entered through the input/edit facility input screens. The authority file consists of author headings (personal, corporate, and conference names), uniform titles, series, and subject headings.

The system uses the ADABAS data base management system. As modified by WLN licensees, the system can handle MARC authority records, but it uses an ADABAS internal format for handling the authority data. The ADABAS format is presently being upgraded to be MARC compatible so that it will contain all MARC fields. The one major drawback of the present format is its inability to contain the authority record control number. This makes automatic changing of the file difficult. In contrast to the MELVYL system, each library in the WLN system can theoretically choose to have authorized headings different from those of other libraries. Furthermore, these authorized headings will be included in the authority file without record redundancy. This is done by identifying authority groups, or groups of libraries that use and share in the maintenance of the same name, subject, and series authority files. The collection-level information for various bibliographic records includes the choice and form of main, added, subject, and series entries and related cross-references. The WLN *Authority Maintenance Manual* (p. 6) explains it this way:

> One of the features of the WLN software is its provision for different "collections," each of which could provide a different view of the same heading. Each collection uses a consistent set of standards for the establishment of authority headings.... Different views of the same authority record do not involve multiple copies of the record. There is still only one authority record with multiple fields, each with a collection "mask" or identifier. Each participant, through its signon, may see its own collection view of a record in its collection. Depending on the application decisions made by the network, the participant may also see a different collection view of a record that is not in the participant's collection. For example, in the initial WLN system, Collection 0 was defined for LC source records and Collection 1 for records input or used by the WLN participants. If a WLN participant displayed a record residing in both Collection 1 and 0, only the Collection 1 view of the record is displayed; if the record is only in Collection 0, the Collection 0 view of the record is displayed. The use of collections in the WLN software reduces the amount of redundancy of records, while allowing flexibility in the application of different authority standards in one network.

Despite this flexibility, the imposition of national standards and the economic reality of accepting such standards essentially precludes much deviation from a given set of heading standards. The ratio of authority records (name and subject) to bibliographic records is almost 1:1 (2,822,873 authority records and 3,225,846 bibliographic records).

Data Base Processing

Authority records are added to the authority file primarily during the processing of bibliographic records. Headings are stripped off the incoming bibliographic records and matched against the existing authority file; if no match exists, an authority record is formed and placed in a file for review by system control personnel.

Quality Control

WLN uses a variety of means to ensure quality control of the data base. These means include intensive training of participants in MARC tagging and input, and human and automatic review at the library and network levels. Access to and/or the ability to modify specific files are under password control; any changes to bibliographic and authority data are automatically reviewed by the bibliographic maintenance staff, who alone have "master access" to all records and files; finally, participants agree to follow specific standards, namely LC choice and form of entry, and subject and descriptive cataloging practices. These standards are enforced by automatic and human review of all newly added records. Machine editing of all records is carried out, checking for MARC format errors such as incorrect tags, invalid tags, invalid subfield codes, nonrepeatable tags or subfield codes, and errors in nonfiling character. indicators. Human review takes place after this machine editing and after records are stored in the individual library's working file.

Public Display/Use

Authority records may be examined from any terminal in the system by entering a series of commands specifying that the given search is an authority search and identifying the type of search desired. Four types of display can be provided for authority records, each giving different types of information.

Evaluation

The system provides several different types of descriptive statistics and diagnostics for evaluation. No other type of evaluation is done at this time.

(Text continues on page 64.)

Table 5.1. Comparative Chart of Authority Systems.

	Class 1	Class 2			Class 3	
	OCLC	RLIN	LC	NYPL	MELVYL	WLN
The Data Base						
1. Data source	LC only	LC NYPL	LC	from bib. rec. LC original input	from bib. rec. LC original input	from bib. rec. LC original input
2. Internal format	modified MARC	MARC	MARC & mnemonics	local format	ADABAS	ADABAS
3. MARC handling capability	full MARC	full MARC	full MARC	partial MARC	full MARC	partial MARC
4. MARC resolution	full	full	full	partial	full	partial
5. Ratio of authority to bibliographic file	1:11	1:6	2:5	1:2	2:1	1:1
Data Base Processing						
6. Addition of new records	yes	yes	yes	yes	yes	yes
7. Method of changing file	automatic	automatic	automatic & manual edit	automatic & manual edit	automatic	manual edit
8. Manual editing	no	no	yes	yes	no	yes
9. 87x fields used to make cross-references	no	no	no	no	no	no

(Table 5.1 continues.)

Table 5.1–*Continued*

| | Class 1 | Class 2 | | | Class 3 | |
	OCLC	RLIN	LC	NYPL	MELVYL	WLN
Quality Control						
10. Error correction for format	yes	yes	yes	yes	yes	yes
11. Error correction for content	yes	yes	yes	yes	yes	yes
12. Review of new headings	no	no	yes	yes	no	yes
13. Developed maintenance routines	no	no	yes	yes	no	yes
14. Security	read only	read only	read only	sign-on codes	read only	passwords
Public Display/Use						
15. Types of formats	mod MARC	MARC	PCRD NCRD	MARC	labeled	4 types
16. Searching of file	4, 3, 1 or 3, 2, 2, 1 types	Boolean	full name & Boolean	full name	Boolean	Boolean
17. Authority form displayed on retrieval	no link	no link	yes, if specified	yes	yes	no
18. Links to circulation system	none	none	none	none	none	none
19. Links to other other files	link to previously searched bibliographic record	none	none	none	none	none

Evaluation

20. Descriptive statistics	yes	yes	yes	yes	yes	yes
21. Feedback from users	error reports only	no	yes	error reports only	no	yes
22. Other evaluative procedures	none	none	none	none	none	none

SUMMARY AND OBSERVATIONS

The Data Base

All of the systems described above and listed in Table 5.1 use the LC MARC authority records to some degree. Although this is not remarkable, it underlines the need for a reliable and consistent source of authority data. It is certainly possible, and the trend seems to be, that more and more libraries will want to create their own authority records and share them, just as they do with bibliographic records. Some type of authority record code is obviously needed to prescribe what information such records should contain and to determine what conventions the recording should follow.

Most of the systems now have or soon will have full MARC handling capability and use or will use the first edition of the authority format.

The one anomaly in this section is the differing ratios of size of authority file to bibliographic file. The significance of this statistic deserves further investigation.

Data Base Processing

All the systems have or plan to have automatic methods of adding new records to the file and changing the file. Those that change the files do so in a batch mode.

Quality Control

All the systems have some mechanism for detecting errors in content designation. Two areas that need further investigation and clarification are the extent to which new headings are reviewed by qualified personnel and the development of maintenance routines. The more complicated these systems become, the greater will be the need for well-thought-out maintenance procedures.

Security does not pose any problem at this time. The systems are, for all intents and purposes, read-only, and except for some WLN licensees, the authority file is not for public use.

Public Display/Use

The systems exhibit the most variety in this area. The types of internal formats, the manner in which they are displayed, and the types of search keys or commands necessary for retrieval all differ from system to system. All this variation works off the same basic information: In none of the systems examined here is the authority system linked in any way to the circulation file.

Evaluation

All the systems provide some degree of descriptive statistics on operations. There is some concern about feedback, but since these systems are not public, serving mainly technical services personnel, this type of evaluation is minimal for the authority file. One reason for this is the lack of control over the creation of authority data in the first place, and the lack of a nationwide code for authority record creation. No other evaluative procedures are carried out, indicating, I believe, our ignorance about the creation, use, and maintenance of authority systems. They are, in their present manifestation, too new.

Other Comments

The most frustrating aspect of a study of this kind is the character and amount of source documentation available. Many systems do not provide accurate and detailed information about their authority system as a whole. Either the emphasis is on the display of the information or on the bibliographic file. WLN is an exception to this rule. It supplies the library community with sufficient information to carry out an adequate assessment of the current state of the system.

Another shortcoming of the source documentation is the tendency of writers to discuss the actual system and the planned system in the same breath. Certainly no duplicity is intended, but writers do often fail to distinguish clearly enough between present and future.

Comparing authority systems on a characteristic-by-characteristic basis is instructive to the potential user and researcher, pointing up similarities and differences that are often not illuminated by the existing literature. A study of this kind also points to the need for further investigation and more abundant documentation, so that the library community may assess adequately and with assurance the existing automated authority systems. Specifically, we need:

1. to know the meaning of the authority-file-to-bibliographic-file ratio;

2. to move toward expanded cooperation beyond the NACO Project in the production of authority data;

3. to develop ways of structuring bibliographic maintenance routines in complex on-line environments; and

4. to determine how in practice use of the authority file helps or hinders retrieval from a bibliographic file.[15]

The fulfillment of these goals will bring us closer to meeting the increasingly complex needs of library users.

NOTES

1. Kazuko M. Dailey, Grazia Jaroff, and Diana Gray, "RLIN and OCLC–Side by Side: Two Comparison Studies," *Advances in Library Administration and Organization* 1:69-125 (1982); Diane Hillman and Christopher Sugnet, "Comparison of OCLC and RLIN: A Question of Quality," *Cataloging and Classification Quarterly* 4(1):65-72 (Fall 1983); Joseph R. Matthews, "Requirements for an On-Line Catalog," *Technicalities* 1(1):11-13 (October 1981); Stephen R. Salmon, "Characteristics of On-Line Public Catalogs," *Library Resources and Technical Services* 27:36-67 (January/March 1983); Joseph R. Matthews and Joan Frye

Williams, "The Bibliographic Utilities, Progress and Problems," *Library Technology Reports* 18(6):609-653 (November/December 1982); and Charles Hildreth, *Online Public Access Catalogs: The User Interface* (Dublin, Ohio: OCLC, 1982).

2.   Robert H. Burger, "Artificial Intelligence and Authority Control," *Library Resources and Technical Services* 28(4):337-345 (October/December 1984).

3.   See, for example, S. Michael Malinconico, "Bibliographic Data Base Organization and Authority File Control," *Wilson Library Bulletin* 54:36-45 (September 1979); Larry Auld, "Authority Control: An Eighty-Year Review," *Library Resources and Technical Services* 26:319-330 (October/December 1982); Helen F. Schmierer, "The Relationship of Authority Control to the Library Catalog," *Illinois Libraries* 62:599-603 (September 1980); and Henriette D. Avram, "Authority Control and Its Place," *Journal of Academic Librarianship* 9(6):331-335 (January 1984).

4.   Arnold Wajenberg and Michael Gorman, "OCLC's Data Base Conversion: A User's Perspective," *Journal of Library Automation* 14(3):174-189 (September 1981).

5.   Council on Library Resources, Inc., Bibliographic Service Development Program, "An Integrated Consistent Authority File Service for Nationwide Use," *Library of Congress Information Bulletin* 39:244-248 (July 11, 1980).

6.   William G. Potter, "When Names Collide: Conflict in the Catalog and AACR2," *Library Resources and Technical Services* 24:3-16 (Winter 1980), and Potter, "Lotka's Law Revisited," *Library Trends* 30(1):21-39 (Summer 1981).

7.   OCLC, *Name Authority: User Manual*, 2nd ed. (Dublin, Ohio: OCLC, 1983), 1.

8.   As of July 1984.

9.   OCLC, *Name Authority*, 3:2-3:3.

10.   Material for this section was taken from the following sources: "RLG's RLIN Authority Subsystem Ready for Searching," *Information Technology and Libraries* 2:218 (June 1983); Research Libraries Group, *RLIN: System Reference Manual*, 1st ed. (Stanford, Calif.: RLG, 1984); and personal communication with Tina Kass, RLIN representative, July 6, 1984.

11.   Material for this section was taken from the following sources: Library of Congress "Descriptive Cataloging Manual," sections N, Z1, and Z2; Library of Congress, Automated Systems Office, *MUMS Reference Guide* (Washington, D.C.: Library of Congress, March 1983); "New Authority System Now Online" *Library of Congress Information Bulletin* 41:313 (October 1, 1982); "MARC Books, Authority Files Contain 2,750,000 Records," *Library of Congress Information Bulletin* 43:15-16 (January 23, 1984); Council on Library Resources, Inc., Bibliographic Service Development Program, "An Integrated Consistent Authority File Service for Nationwide Use," *Library of Congress Information Bulletin* 39:244-248 (July 11, 1980); personal communication with Suzanne Liggett and Judy Fenley, NACO Project, and Ann Della Porta, Shared Cataloging Division, Library of Congress; and "Library Verifies 500,000th Name Authority Record," *Library of Congress Information Bulletin* 40:54-55 (February 13, 1981).

12.   Material for this section was obtained from the following sources: New York Public Library, *ONLICATS: System Reference Manual*, distributed by New York Public Library, Library Information & On-Line Network Systems (n.d.); and personal communication with Walter Grutchfield, manager of systems development, New York Public Library, July 27, 1983, and July 6, 1984.

13.   Material for this section was obtained from the following sources: Barbara S. Radke, Katharina E. Klemperer, and Michael G. Berger, "The User-Friendly Catalog: Patron Access to MELVYL," *Information Technology and Libraries* 1:358-371 (December 1982); Ray R. Larson and Vicki Graham, "Monitoring and Evaluating MELVYL," *Information Technology and Libraries* 2:93-104 (March 1983); Dorothy McPherson, *Authority Control in the University of California Union Catalog,* Division of Library Automation Working Paper 9 (Berkeley, Calif.: Division of Library Automation, Office of the Assistant Vice President, Library Plans and Policies, University of California, May 1979, rev. October 1980); unpublished memorandum from Dorothy McPherson to Joe Rosenthal, "DLA Authority System Changes to Campus Headings," March 24, 1983; and personal communication with Dorothy McPherson, July 2, 1984.

14.   Material for this section was obtained from the following sources: Washington Library Network, *Authority Reference Manual,* 2nd draft (Olympia, Wash.: Washington State Library, April 1979); Washington Library Network, *Authority Maintenance Manual for Applications of WLN Software,* draft (Olympia, Wash.: Washington State Library, December 1982); Jo Calk, "On-Line Authority Control in the Washington Library Network," in *What's in a Name: Control of Catalogue Records through Automated Authority Files,* ed. and comp. Natsuko Furuya (Toronto: University of Toronto Press, 1978); Gwen Culp, "Authority Control Within the Washington Library Network Computer System," in *Authority Control: The Key to Tomorrow's Catalog* ed. Mary W. Ghikas (Phoenix, Ariz.: Oryx Press, 1982); Richard Woods, "The Washington Library Network Computer System," *Online Review* 3(3):297-330 (1979); and personal communication with Robert D. Payne, WLN representative, July 19, 1983, and with Heather Nicoll, WLN representative, July 16, 1984.

15.   For an example of such research, see Arlene G. Taylor, "Authority Files in Online Catalogs: An Investigation of Their Value," *Cataloging and Classification Quarterly* 4(3):1-17 (Spring 1984).

6

CONCLUSION

FUTURE TRENDS

Three major trends will affect authority control over the next several years: (1) the increase in the number of sources of authority data, (2) the appearance of agencies performing tasks that support authority control, and (3) the increase in retrospective conversion projects.

In 1940 the Library of Congress started a program called Cooperative Cataloging.[1] Under this program, selected libraries were asked to submit bibliographic records to the Library of Congress for inclusion in the National Union Catalog. These records were to be prepared according to strict guidelines given to the participating libraries.

These libraries were also to prepare authority cards for

> a main or secondary entry not known to be already represented on Library of Congress or cooperatively printed cards, ... on special [yellow] stock which is supplied, upon request, by the Cooperative Cataloging Section, and forwarded with the copy to which it belongs. Because the authority card is to be inserted into the Official Catalog at the Library of Congress, it should be prepared according to current practice of the Descriptive Cataloging Division of the Library of Congress, listing the authorities consulted, using abbreviations from the list of more common reference sources ... and carrying appropriate checks for identification.[2]

Since 1977 an analogous project, the Name Authority Cooperative (NACO) Project has been under way. This project, which currently involves thirty-four cooperating libraries, has developed along lines similar to the Cooperative Cataloging project. Cooperating libraries submit authority records, on LC forms, for names that do not yet exist in the file of MARC authority records. Some of the cooperating libraries, those that for some time have been producing high-quality records in above-average quantities, have dial-up access to the LC data base of authority and bibliographic records. Other libraries access the MARC authority records through their membership in a primary network (RLIN, OCLC).

Each library is required to follow the appropriate chapters of the LC "Descriptive Cataloging Manual," as well as the LC RIs. Before submission to the Library of Congress, all names are checked against the on-line file of authority records to eliminate duplication. A new member's records are scrutinized individually until such time as the error rate is judged acceptably low. At this time "independent" status is granted, and thenceforth only samples of the contributing library's records are reviewed. By this process, the Library of Congress promotes the submission of new records and yet keeps sufficient control over the submissions to maintain the high-quality records for which the library has become known.

This project signals a trend that is likely to continue—the creation and distribution beyond the creating library of authority records for use by other libraries, in much the same way bibliographic records are created and distributed today. What remains to be established is a commonly accepted set of standards for recording and distribution. The Z chapters of the LC "Descriptive Cataloging Manual," which deal with procedures for the creation and change of authority records, and the procedures in force with the NACO Project will obviously play a major role in this development.[3]

An example of the second major trend, the appearance of agencies performing tasks that support authority control, is the AMIGOS Bibliographic Council in Dallas, Texas. AMIGOS receives bibliographic records in machine-readable form and runs the headings from those tapes against the current MARC authority file. When a match is encountered with a cross-reference, AMIGOS substitutes the currently authorized heading for the form on the tapes. This type of service is especially helpful for libraries and networks with a large backlog of machine-readable bibliographic records that need to be "cleaned up" before they are loaded into a newly developed on-line catalog. This type of activity will surely expand over the coming years.

The third major trend, the increase in retrospective conversion projects, is closely related to the second.[4] One of the problems in retrospective conversion is achieving uniformity of headings in both the converted former card or book file and the more recent records that may have been created according to updated standards. The demand by converting libraries for a clean file with up-to-date headings and embedded cross-references will force providers of these services to deliver a more acceptable product that contains current authorized headings.

FUTURE CONTEXT

These presently visible developments depend on another vision of the future, the exact context of which is not entirely clear at this time. A national-level network will link the major primary networks, allowing the exchange of bibliographic, authority, and other library-related records. Formats for machine-readable bibliographic records and authority records have already been published in preliminary editions. The Linked Systems Project has made impressive progress, and it will undoubtedly be fully operational in the near future.[5]

While this system will certainly be a dominant force in molding the authority control of the future, other factors will have an impact on this context. Four factors are likely to play a major role.

The first factor is a change in the concept of authority control in a developed machine system.[6] Whether the change is implemented as described in the literature is not as important as the effect this literature has had on our way of conceiving of authority records and systems. Behind this change in concept is, of course, the computer and the possibility it has given of configuring files in the ways described previously (see pp. 7-9).

The second factor is the challenge of the consistent application of rules in a multiinstitutional environment. Cataloging and the application of rules in determining the forms of names is an interpretative activity, one that requires more than literacy and experience in cataloging. Unless one cataloger can easily accept the work of another, the entire concept of a national-level network will be hard to realize. More research is needed into the ways current rules and rule interpretations are formed, used, and interpreted by practicing catalogers and the ways in which patrons search for the names so formed.[7] Inconsistency is a problem that will plague the library community for years to come and obviously cannot be solved overnight. But recognition that there is indeed a problem is urgently needed.

The third factor is an entire set of international implications that have not yet been recognized. Computer-to-computer communication between countries is increasing. Besides the sharing of bibliographic descriptions that is just beginning to take shape in earnest, the sharing of authority records is likely to develop. The conflict between national policies that demand adherence to standards, extra paperwork, etc., and cost effectiveness and retrievability will surely be a relevant issue in authority control in the years ahead.

The fourth factor is the development of evaluation mechanisms for future and current machine systems. Chapter 4 touched upon some evaluative mechanisms that need to be explored. With such evaluation will come increased information about how authority systems operate and where they fail. Such feedback will directly affect authority work and authority control in the future.

NECESSARY RESEARCH ON AUTHORITY WORK

Some areas in which research is needed, such as the ways rules and rule interpretations are formed, used, and interpreted by practicing catalogers, have been mentioned above. But there are other areas that may not be as readily perceivable. We also need:

1. details about the history of authority work in this country and abroad

2. a more rigorous definition of the term *access point*

3. more sophisticated and streamlined processes by which authority control can be carried out

4. surveys on the ways authority systems are used and who uses them

5. more developed ways of evaluating authority systems and of conveying the results to library managers, so that they may make better decisions with regard to processing as a whole

6. an understanding of the meaning of the ratio of authority file size to bibliographic file size

7. empirical studies that will reveal the best way of controlling the quality of the authority file

8. efficient ways of developing maintenance procedures for authority systems

9. evidence for how in practice use of the authority file helps or hinders retrieval from a bibliographic file

Authority work is a central part of cataloging and therefore of library use in general. Technological and economic developments will affect authority work in ways that cannot be clearly foreseen. The best way to be prepared for such a future is to be thoroughly grounded in the principles of all aspects of authority work. This book is a first step in that preparation.

NOTES

1. Library of Congress, Descriptive Cataloging Division, *Cooperative Cataloging Manual for the Use of Contributing Libraries* (Washington, D.C.: Government Printing Office, 1944).

2. Ibid., 27.

3. Library of Congress, "Descriptive Cataloging Manual," Chapter N1, 1-2.

4. Robert H. Burger, "Conversion of Cataloging Records to Machine-Readable Form: Major Projects, Continuing Problems, and Future Prospects," *Cataloging and Classification Quarterly* 3:27-40 (Fall 1982); Brett Butler, Brian Aveney, and William Scholz, "The Conversion of Manual Catalogs to Collection Data Bases," *Library Technology Reports* 14(2) (March-April 1978); and Ruth C. Carter and Scott Bruntjen, *Data Conversion* (White Plains, N.Y.: Knowledge Industry Publications, 1983).

5. Wayne E. Davison, "The WLN/RLG/LC Linked Systems Project," *Information Technology and Libraries* 2:34-36 (March 1983); and Council on Library Resources, Inc., Bibliographic Service Development Program, Task Force on a Name Authority File Service, *The Name Authority Cooperative/Name Authority File Service* (Washington, D.C.: Council on Library Resources, May 1984).

6. Michael Gorman, "Authority Files in a Developed Machine System (With Particular Reference to AACR II)," in *What's in a Name: Control of Catalogue Records through Automated Authority Files,* ed. and comp. Natsuko Y. Furuya (Toronto: University of Toronto Press, 1978); and Michael Gorman and Robert H. Burger, "Serial Control in a Developed Machine System," *Serials Librarian* 5(1):13-26 (Spring 1982).

7. Arlene G. Taylor, "Authority Files in Online Catalogs: An Investigation of Their Value," *Cataloging and Classification Quarterly* 4(3):1-17.

APPENDIX: MACHINE-READABLE NAME AUTHORITY FORMAT

The American library community has been receiving standardized bibliographic data from the Library of Congress since 1901. It was not until 1977, however, that standardized authority data began to be similarly distributed.

The three most important reasons for the appearance of machine-readable authority data were:

1. the increasing emphasis of cataloging codes on the form of entries

2. the increasing use by libraries of machine-readable bibliographic data

3. the development and broadening application of the MARC format for bibliographic records

The history of the MARC format has been fully chronicled elsewhere, but a brief sketch of the development of the standardized format for transmission of bibliographic records (the MARC format) will be helpful in understanding the background and context of the MARC format for authority records.

In 1964 the MARC Development Office was formed at the Library of Congress in order to "test the feasibility of a distribution service of centrally produced machine-readable cataloging data."[1] The MARC pilot project lasted for two years. In 1968, after LC staff members had consulted with cataloging experts outside the Library of Congress, the MARC II format was adopted by the American Library Association (ALA) as the official U.S. format. The MARC II format was also adopted by the American National Standards Institute (ANSI) as ANSI Z39.2-1971 and has since been updated to an implementation of ANSI Z39.2-1979, the *American National Standard for Information Interchange on Magnetic Tape.* Finally, it has also been issued and adopted by the International Standards Organization (ISO) as ISO-2709-1981, the *Documentation-Format for Bibliographic Information Interchange on Magnetic Tape.* The MARC II format is now referred to as the US/MARC format.[2] Since 1968 several other countries have developed their own MARC formats, the United Kingdom being the first to do so. Over the past fifteen years, there have been several attempts to make these various national MARC formats compatible.[3]

Initially, only the book format was defined. Six other formats for bibliographic records have now been developed, for films, manuscripts, maps, music and sound recordings, serials, and machine-readable data files. An eighth format, the one for authority records, is the subject of this appendix. It is not surprising that the MARC format for authority records has been a relative latecomer to the MARC format family. When the MARC II version of the bibliographic format was developed, some libraries and several automated centers could use machine-readable bibliographic data. Few, including the Library of Congress itself, had use in the late 1960s and early 1970s for machine-readable authority records.

The distinction between bibliographic records and authority records has been discussed. Because these two types of records are essentially different, because they serve different purposes and are therefore functionally different, the formats for bibliographic and authority records differ as well. Before proceeding to a detailed examination of the MARC authority format, it would be wise to consider the seemingly abstract notion of the definition of a format and its use.

It might be expected that the definition of a format would be fairly old hat by now, after fifteen years of library automation. Yet recently a member of the Machine Representation of Bibliographic Information (MARBI) committee, John Attig, pointed to the necessity of finally providing such a definition. As a matter of fact, Attig has claimed that the meaning of the term *format* is "the most significant issue facing the authors of the US/MARC formats."[4] His suggested definition of *format* reads: "A distinct set of content designators prescribed for the identification and characterization of data in a type of MARC record. Separate formats should be defined for types of records that are mutually exclusive and distinct in function—such as authority and bibliographic records."[5] On the basis of this definition, it is clear that the authority format is one of the two types of formats that now exist. Fortunately for our purposes, much of the controversy today over the use of machine-readable bibliographic and authority data revolves around the several bibliographic formats that exist and the desire to produce one unified bibliographic format.[6]

As with the MARC bibliographic format, there was a preliminary version of the authority format. In 1976, the Library of Congress issued *Authorities: A MARC Format: Specifications for Magnetic Tapes Containing Authority Records,* preliminary edition. In the document's Introduction, the authors state the purpose and scope of the format: "The MARC authority record format provides specifications and content designators for name, uniform title, and subject authorities. Other kinds of authorities such as series could be accommodated by this format, but provisions for specific fields or codes have not been made, pending further analysis."[7]

From 1976 to 1981, addenda were issued to the preliminary edition. During this time, machine-readable authority records were distributed to customers throughout the United States and Europe. In 1981, the first edition of *Authorities: A MARC Format* appeared, superseding the preliminary edition with addenda. Its statement of purpose and function differs from the preliminary edition:

> The MARC authorities format provides specifications for the content and the content designation of authority records containing name, subject, and/or series authority information based on the ALA *Rules for Author and Title Entries,* the *Anglo-American Cataloguing Rules* [AACR 1 and 2] and the Library of Congress Subject Headings.

The authorities format is designed to accommodate in a single record all of the authority information pertinent to the use of a given heading as a name and/or a subject and/or a series. However, a separate authority record may be created for each different application (name, subject, or series) of the same heading.[8]

Note that the first edition does contain authority information for series, whereas the preliminary edition did not. Two other differences, which will be discussed below, are that control subfield $w has been redefined and narrowed in use and that record-level transaction date/time information has superseded field-level transaction date/time information.

GENERAL STRUCTURE OF THE RECORD

Like its bibliographic relation, the authority format consists structurally of four parts: leader, record directory, control fields, and variable fields. All of the content of the authority record—the authority information—as well as information about the character of the record itself is contained in one of these four parts. The authority record can be thought of as a string of numbers, alphabetic characters, and special symbols. Each of the four parts, as well as individual control and variable field, is separated from the others within the record. An examination of the individual parts of the record follows.

The Leader

The leader is always twenty-four characters long. The positions of the characters are numbered from 0 to 23, and the characters are grouped into nine data elements. The leader provides parameters for pieces of information that are used for the processing of the record. (See Figure A.1, p. 76, and Table A.1, p. 77.) Each character position is then further defined within the authority format. For example, the definition of logical record length (bytes 0-4) reads: "The logical record length is computer-generated; it is the total number of characters in the logical record, including the length itself. The number is right justified with zero fill."[9]

(Text continues on page 78.)

$$
\begin{array}{c}
\overset{1}{\overbrace{\quad}}\ \ \overset{2\ 3}{|\ |}\ \ \overset{4}{\overbrace{\ }}\ \ \overset{5}{\overbrace{\ }}\ \ \overset{6}{\overbrace{\quad}}\ \ \overset{7\ 8}{|\ }\ \ \overset{9}{\overbrace{\quad}} \\
\emptyset\ \emptyset\ 3\ 5\ \emptyset\ n\ z\ \text{b}\ \text{b}\ \text{b}\ 2\ 2\ \emptyset\ \emptyset\ \emptyset\ 6\ 1\ n\ \text{b}\ \text{b}\ 4\ 5\ \emptyset\ \emptyset \\
0\qquad\quad 5\qquad\qquad 10\qquad\qquad 15\qquad\qquad 20\quad 23
\end{array}
$$

character positions

Key

b —blank

∅ —zero

1—length of logical record (350 bytes here)

2—status (code n means new record)

3—type of record (code z signifies authority data)

4—these bytes are always blanks

5—indicator and subfield code count; in the **MARC** format both positions are always 2

6—base address; starting position of first control field (byte 61 here)

7—encoding level (code n indicates complete authority data)

8—these bytes are always blanks

9—entry map; in **MARC** format these values are always 4500

Figure A.1. Example of a leader.

Table A.1.
Outline of the Leader.

Leader data element	Number of characters	Character position in leader
Logical record length	5	0-4
Record status	1	5
Legend		
Type of record	1	6
Blanks	3	7-9
Indicator count	1	10
Subfield code count	1	11
Base address of data	5	12-16
Encoding level	1	17
Blanks	2	18-19
Entry map (map of record directory entries)		
Length of the length-of-field part	1	20
Length of the starting-character part	1	21
Length of the implementation-defined part	1	22
Undefined character	1	23

As stated previously, the information contained in the leader is used primarily by programmers to process machine-readable authority data. The leader can also be important to the librarian assigned to draw up specifications for the processing of the authority file. As more and more libraries use machine-readable authority data, a growing number of librarians will be required to know intimately the innards of this and other formats. It will be the librarian who draws up specifications for the programmer to follow. In this regard, it is important to point out one of the most important bytes in the leader, byte 5, record status.

The definition of this byte consists primarily of the codes used in the byte and their meanings. Codes and meanings are listed below.

a—increase in encoding level

b—corrected or revised record

d—record deleted because heading has been replaced by another heading

n—new record

s—record deleted because heading has been split into two or more headings

x—record deleted (explanation may be present in field 682)

"Value 'd' is used when the record is deleted and replaced by a new authority record in which the heading from the deleted record appears as a tracing in a 4xx field."[10]

According to the policy established by the first edition of the authority format, when a record is corrected or changed, an entirely new record is issued. Prior to 1984, when the preliminary edition was in use, records were changed or corrected by the issue of a corrected record. The fact that a record was a corrected one would be indicated in byte 5 of the leader. In addition, there was a complex and cumbersome way of indicating within the record what information was new and what had been deleted. The handful of users of the preliminary edition found this method of processing changed records so difficult to use and discovered so many mistakes in the processing of the records that they successfully urged the method be discontinued. The existing codes for byte 5 indicate flexibility of use for the machine-readable record, depending on future use of the first edition.

In summary, those writing specifications for authority records will find byte 5 useful as a flag for indicating a new or corrected record and then can route the record to the appropriate subroutine in the processing system for appropriate action.

The Record Directory

The record directory is the second of the four main parts of the machine-readable authority record. It is used exclusively in the machine processing of the record and is unlikely to be used by librarians who write specifications for use of these records. The record directory consists of several fixed-length sections, each of which corresponds to a control or a variable field in the record itself. Each entry is twelve characters, or bytes, long and consists of three parts—a code for the tag, the field length, and the starting-character position of each field within the record. Table A.2 gives the name, length, and position of each data element,[11] and an example follows. At present all the characters in the record directory are numeric.

Table A.2.
Outline of a Record Directory Entry.

Record directory data element	Number of characters	Character position in directory
Tag	3	0-2
Field length	4	3-6
Starting-character position	5	7-11

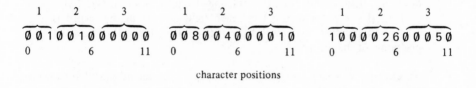

character positions

Key

1—tag

2—field length

3—starting-character position

The tag "is a three-character numeric symbol that identifies a field."[12] Tags can range from 001 to 899 *in this format*, although at present many of these potential values are unassigned. Generally speaking, the order in which tags appear in the record, and thus in the record directory, is strictly numerical. The exception to this rule is the tags for the 4xx and 5xx fields, in which entries are grouped by the first digit of the tag and, within these two groups, by the order in which they appear in the record, an order that is not always strictly numerical.

The field length is the length in bytes, or characters, of the field identified by the tag. This count includes the following elements of such an entry (the individual parts will be discussed below under Variable Fields, p. 88): indicators, subfield codes, data, and a field terminator. This number is right justified with zero fill. This means that if the field length were 15, bytes 3 through 6 would look like this: Ø Ø 1 5. Similarly, if the field length were 1200, bytes 3 through 6 would look like this: 1 2 Ø Ø.

For processing purposes, the crucial question is "Where does the starting-character position begin?" Bytes 12 through 16 of the leader answer the question. The definition given in the format is concise and to the point:

> The base address of data, which is the starting-character position of the first control field, gives the base from which each field is addressed. The number is right justified with zero fill. It is equal to the sum of the lengths of the leader and the record directory, including the record directory field terminator. The starting-character position (see bytes 7-11 of the record directory) for each field entered in the record is relative to the first character of the first control field rather than the beginning of the record.[13]

An example will help to clarify this concept. Each record must have a leader twenty-four characters (bytes 1 through 23) long. Since it is defined this way, the leader does not have a special character at the end to signal that the leader has ended. The leader is immediately followed by the record directory, a series of twelve-character sections, each section consisting of data for each individual record entry. This sequence of twelve-character sections ends with a special character called a field terminator, which signals that the record directory has ended. The number of sections in each record directory will vary according to the record processed. However, it may never have less than three such entries, for the 001 field, the 008 field, and a 1xx field.

Control Fields

Control fields "contain numbers, dates, and codes which specify characteristics of the record and/or the heading, and which are intended primarily for computer processing of an authority file."[14] Each control field is identified by a three-character numeric tag with two leading zeroes. The current control field tags are 001, 002, 005, and 008. As stated earlier in this chapter, all of the tags in the range 001 through 899 have not yet been identified, and some are not currently used. Brief explanations of fields 001, 002, and 005 follow. Field 008, because of its importance in processing and specification writing, receives fuller treatment.

001—Authority Record Control Number

This field contains the authority control number assigned by the organization that creates the authority record. The field is not repeatable and may occur only once in the record. This is not a fixed-length field, but as the Library of Congress has defined its use for its own authority control number, certain character positions in the field have specific meanings. Table A.3 gives the names, length, and position of the data elements.

Table A.3.
Outline of Authority Record Control Number.

Name of data element	Number of characters	Character position in field
Alphabetic prefix	3	0-2
Year	2	3-4
Serial number	6	5-10
Supplement number	1	11
Alphabetic identifier and/or revision date	variable	12-

A typical LC authority control number is nbbb83167642b. The control number in the authority record is similar to the control number in the bibliographic format, but it contains one of two prefixes. Name authority records contain the prefix n; subject authority records contain the prefix sh. The two year characters represent the year the record was created in machine-readable form. If, however, the record has not been input at the Library of Congress but has been converted from the Library's existing authority file by another agency acting under contract to the Library, the prefix is 50 or 42 instead of the year—50 for name authorities and 42 for series authorities. The serial number is a sequentially assigned number of from one to six digits. The supplement number currently contains a blank (portrayed as b in this book); it was included to conform with the bibliographic record. The alphabetic identifier and/or revision date has also been included in order to conform with the bibliographic record. It is not currently used.

It is possible for a personal name, or more likely a geographic name, to have one authority record with an n prefix and another with a sh prefix. The extent to which this occurs is unknown, but it does occur. Part of the reason is the logical possibility that a given name could perform two different functions in the catalog, as responsible party (name authority) and as subject (subject authority). In some cases, two different authority records may be created by the different divisions at the Library of Congress that produce such records, the descriptive cataloging department and the subject cataloging department.

002—Subrecord Linkage Field

This field, reserved to present subrecord relationships, is not used at present.

005—Date and Time of Latest Transaction

This nonrepeatable field shows the date and time of the latest change in or addition to the record or of the creation of the record itself. It is a fixed-length field consisting of sixteen characters, each of which must be numeric. The date information is recorded according to the *American National Standard Representations for Calendar Date and Ordinal Date for Information Interchange.* The time is shown in accordance with the *American National Standard Representations of Local Time of the Day for Information Interchange.* The field is divided evenly into two sections of eight characters each. The date section records the date thus: four characters for the year, two for the month, and two for the day. The time section uses two characters for the hour, two for the minute, two for the second, and two for a decimal fraction at the second, including the decimal point. For example, the date and time September 2, 1981, 2:12:36 (2 p.m., 12 minutes and 36 seconds) would be rendered: 19810902141236.0.

008—Fixed-Length Data Elements

Perhaps the most important control field is the 008 field. It is of fixed length and contains forty characters. Each position is defined for specific information. Some of the character positions have not been defined and they contain blanks. The names, length, and position of the data elements of this field are shown in Table A.4. It would be sadistic to define for the reader each of the nineteen codes in the field. Rather, let us focus clearly on some of the more important codes and discuss uses in specification writing for some of them.

Table A.4.
Outline of Fixed-Length Data Elements.

Data element	Number of characters	Character position in field
Date entered on file	6	0-5
Direct/indirect geographic subdivision code	1	6

Table A.4–*Continued*

Data element	Number of characters	Character position in field
Romanization scheme	1	7
Blank	1	8
Authority/reference record code	1	9
Cataloging rules code	1	10
Subject heading system code	1	11
Type of series code	1	12
Numbered/unnumbered series code	1	13
Heading use code—main or added entry	1	14
Heading use code—subject-added entry	1	15
Heading use code—series-added entry	1	16
Blanks	11	17-27
Type of government agency code	1	28
Reference evaluation code	1	29
Blank	1	30
Record update in process code	1	31
Undifferentiated personal name code	1	32
Status of authority heading code	1	33
Blank	1	34
Language of heading code	3	35-37
Modified record code	1	38
Cataloging source code	1	39

Date Entered on File (Bytes 0-5)

This code shows the date the record was entered into the LC authority file. If the record is changed the date remains the same, unless the record undergoes "extensive revision."[15] This date is useful for identifying obsolete records that may not have been deleted from a local file and for determining under what policies the heading was created.

Authority/Reference Record Code (Byte 9)

This character indicates whether the record is an authority record or a reference record. In the doublespeak of machine-readable authority records, a reference record is not an authority record, but it is an authority record. That is, authority records are of two types, authority records and reference records. At present the following codes apply:

a—authority record

b—reference record (untraced reference)

c—reference record (traced reference)

Authority records contain a 1xx field that is an established heading. Reference records contain a 1xx field that is not an established form of heading. For name authorities, reference records are cataloger-generated references, for example, for two or more authors who also publish under a joint pseudonym. This subtle distinction will be made clearer below under the section References and Tracings, p. 97.

Cataloging Rules Code (Byte 10)

This is one of the most important byte positions in the entire record. It indicates the cataloging rules used in establishing the form of the name heading. At present the following codes apply:

a—early rules (e.g., ALA *Cataloging Rules for Author and Title Entries*)

b—AACR1

c—AACR2

d—non-AACR2 form, but AACR2-compatible heading

e-m, o-z—to be assigned to other rules, as required.

n—not applicable (i.e., heading is not a name)[16]

For this format, new name headings are coded c or d and subject headings are coded n.

Subject Heading System Code (Byte 11)

This byte is especially useful for systems such as WLN that have an internal set of codes corresponding with the values given here. This makes a straightforward transference of codes easier. The following codes are applicable:

a—Library of Congress

b—LC Children's Literature

c—National Library of Medicine

d—National Agricultural Library

k—National Library of Canada English Headings

v—National Library of Canada French Headings

z—other

n—not applicable

Type of Series Code (Byte 12)

This one-character alphabetic code indicates the type of series a heading represents. Examples are:

a—monographic series

b—multipart item

c—series-like phrase not to be considered a series

z—other

n—not applicable

Of course, these single-phrase definitions are elaborated upon in the format instructions themselves. As authority records are used in the more relational data bases of the future,[17] this byte may increase in importance and contain more codes.

Numbered/Unnumbered Series Code (Byte 13)

As is clear from its title, this byte states whether the series is numbered or unnumbered. Any good serials cataloger knows that in the imperfect if not insane world of serials, these are not the only two possibilities. Aside from the code n (not applicable), the code c has significance here—it connotes a series that has been both numbered and unnumbered at different times in its history.[18] The fact that a series is numbered or not determines whether it is possible to trace the series. It is not the sole determinant, but it is a significant characteristic.

Reference Evaluation Code (Byte 29)

According to present LC policy, this byte will be used "for tracings associated with name headings until all tracings on name authority records created prior to the implementation of AACR2 in 1981 have been evaluated and the authority records updated."[19] That is, since the Library of Congress adopted AACR2 on January 1, 1981, for use in the creation of name headings, records created prior to that date may not be AACR2 headings and may have cross-references not in AACR2 form, even if the heading has been changed to AACR2 form. The Library of Congress will review the headings already created and certify whether they are now approved AACR2 headings with AACR2-form references. This is only done on an as-encountered basis; there is currently no program to convert all noncoded headings to AACR2. Present codes are as follows:

a—tracings have not been evaluated and are consistent with the heading

b—tracings have not been evaluated and are not necessarily consistent

n—not applicable

Undifferentiated Personal Name Code (Byte 32)

This code is especially designed to deal with a cataloging policy nightmare. Occasionally it happens that two people who are authors have the same name. The person determining the form of name for use can frequently distinguish between two such people by adding their birth or death dates, a phrase explaining the subject matter of the author's works, and other qualifiers. However, sometimes there is no feasible way to distinguish between the two authors. When identical names cannot be differentiated, the same authority record is used for both names. The following codes are applicable:

a—differentiated personal name

b—undifferentiated personal name

n—not applicable (i.e., not a personal name heading)

All authority records for nonpersonal names are coded n.[20]

Status of Authority Heading Code (Byte 33)

This code should not be confused with leader byte 17 (encoding level), which relates to the fullness of the entire record. This code refers to the 1xx field. It specifies the "level of establishment" or authoritativeness of the heading. The following list of codes will provide a clear picture of the concept of "level of establishment."

a—fully established heading that has been used on a bibliographic record

b—memorandum (heading is established but has not been used on a bibliographic record). This type of authority record is often referred to in systems as an "orphan" record, i.e., one that is not linked to any bibliographic record. It is created when an LC cataloger does research to establish a heading but then finds that the heading will not be used as an access point for the work being cataloged. In order to save others from repeating the work done on the authority record for that heading, the record is saved as a memorandum.

c—provisional (heading cannot be established definitively due to inadequate information; when the heading is next used, it should be reconsidered in the light of any additional information). An example of this occurs in Soviet republican academies of science. Often specific institutes' names are not given in the vernacular language of the academy (Georgian, Kazakh, Uzbek, etc.), but only in Russian. The name is then established using the Russian form, with the qualifier in the vernacular language. When the vernacular form of the institute is found, the record will be upgraded to a fully established heading.

d—preliminary (heading is established in connection with the cataloging of a bibliographic item that is not available at the time the heading is established; the heading will be reconsidered when an appropriate item is available)

n—not applicable (the record is a reference record, not an authority record, and therefore the 1xx field does not contain a valid heading)

There is a relationship between the codes in byte 17 of the leader and byte 33 of the 008 field. The relationship of the codes can best be expressed in tabular form:

if byte 17 has code	then byte 33 of 008 must be
n	any defined code
o	a (normally)

(Code o is an authority record that does not contain complete authority data.) As the parenthetical "normally" reveals, there is always an exception to golden rules in cataloging.

When the heading in the authority record is used for LC cataloging, the code will be a or c. Headings established for records contributed to the National Union Catalog will be coded d. These d codes will be changed to a or c if the headings are used by the Library of Congress in conjunction with a record cataloged by the Library.[21]

Language of Heading Code (Bytes 35-37)

The language of the heading is identified by the appropriate three-character MARC language code. A list of these codes is published as Appendix II.C of *MARC Formats for Bibliographic Data.*[22]

Cataloging Source Code (Byte 39)

This one-character code identifies the source of the authority data and is used in conjunction with field 040 (see Cataloging Source, p. 91).
The codes are:

blank or ƀ—Library of Congress

d—other sources

u—unknown

If code d is present, the National Union Catalog (NUC) symbol of the contributing institution is recorded in subfield $a of field 040. A list of these symbols is available in each chronological series of the National Union Catalog. Under the NACO Project, records contributed by institutions other than the Library of Congress have code d in position 39 and carry the NUC symbol of the contributor in subfield $a of 040 and the LC symbol in subfield $c of the 040. This is analogous to the practice followed with respect to the 040 field in the bibliographic formats.

Variable Fields

The remainder of the fields in the record are variable-length fields. There are five groups of such fields, identified by their tags.

010-090—bibliographic control numbers and codes

100-151—headings

260-551—references and tracings

640-646—series treatment information

663-682—notes

Elements Common to Variable Fields

Besides having tags, like the fixed-length fields, and variable lengths, the variable fields have other common characteristics—indicators, subfield codes, and field terminators.

Indicators

Each variable field begins with a tag, and the indicators follow. These two characters are "intended to control the sorting/filing, construction of search keys, aspects of display, and other machine functions with respect to the data in the field."[23] The description of the indicators defined for each field is included with the description of the entire field. In some cases no indicators are defined and the indicator positions are blanks.

Subfield Codes

Variable fields contain data, and this data is often separated into more than one element. Each element of data is separated from another element of data within a field by a two-character subfield code, consisting of a delimiter—$1F_{16}$ in the eight-bit ASCII character set and 37_8 in the six-bit ASCII, which is in nonstandard set I—and a lower-case alphabetic or numerical character. This two-character code precedes the data element it identifies. Description of each variable field includes descriptions of the subfields as well as the codes applicable to it. In this book, the first character of a subfield code will be represented by a $.

Data

This common element may seem so obvious as not to be worth mentioning. However, conceptually, it is wise to think about data as a common element.[24] The data common to all these fields is that gathered from bibliographic records and reference sources themselves, as well as from systems of control (in the assignment of control numbers) in the Library of Congress. The prescriptive rules for the content of this data lie outside the format, which is only designed to communicate the data in a commonly intelligible form. The data from a name established in 1912 as well as a name established under the present cataloging rules will fit into the format. The format does nothing more than *identify* what data is contained in a specific variable field.

Field Terminator

Each field is separated from the next field in the record by a field terminator. All variable fields end with one. (In the eight-bit ASCII character set the field terminator is $1E_{16}$. In six-bit ASCII the field terminator is 36_8, which is in nonstandard set I.)

In the last variable field of each record, the field terminator is followed by a record terminator, which conforms to ANSI Z39.2-1979. In records distributed by the Library of Congress in the preliminary edition of the format, however, the record terminator replaces the field terminator in the last variable field of a record.[25] (In eight-bit ASCII the record terminator is $1D_{16}$. In six-bit ASCII the record terminator is 35_8, which is in nonstandard set I.)

Variable Fields 010-090

LC Authority Record Control Number (010)

This field contains the control number assigned by the Library of Congress. When another system uses and/or distributes an LC authority record, the local system's record control number is contained in field 001 and the LC number is switched to this field. Field 010 contains two subfields, $a and $z. Subfield $a contains the LC authority record control number, and subfield $z contains a cancelled or invalid LC authority record control number.[26]

Link to Bibliographic Record for Serial or Multi-Part Item (Series) (014)

This field is useful in systems where the authority records and the bibliographic records form separate files; it enables the two records to be linked. Caution should be exercised, however, to ensure that the control number appearing here is structured exactly as in field 001 of the bibliographic record, so that the same logic may be used in the sorting and retrieving of both records. Note that this is a linking field for serials and series *only*.[27]

International Standard Book Number (Series) (020)

This field contains the International Standard Book Number (ISBN) for a multipart item. (An ISBN is a unique identification number assigned to an individual publication.) The number is carried in the record without hyphens or spaces and without the prefix ISBN, which may be generated as a print constant in any system. Indicators are blanks; subfield codes are:

a—ISBN

c—terms of availability (price)

z—canceled/invalid ISBN[28]

International Standard Serial Number (Series) (022)

This field is not mandatory, but when present it carries the International Standard Serial Number (ISSN) for the series of which it is the authorized heading. The prefix ISSN, like the ISBN in field 020, is not carried within the record but may be generated by any system as a print constant for this field. The inclusion of the ISSN in the authority record is one way of linking bibliographic records that have used a heading from a given authority record with that authority record. The ISSN is contained in subfield $a. Subfield $y is used for an incorrect ISSN, and subfield $z for a canceled ISSN. The subfield code $y is also used when the ISSN on an item "is known to vary from the ISSN assigned by the ISDS (International Serials Data System) Center."[29]

Local System Control Number (035)

This field is used to contain a control number that is not the same as that used in fields 001 and 010. It always must be preceded by the NUC symbol of the institution assigning the number. The structure and length of the number are not restricted, except for the prefix. The field contains only one subfield, $a.[30]

Cataloging Source (040)

This field has the same structure and content as the 040 field in bibliographic records. It contains, in appropriate subfields, the NUC symbol of the cataloging agency, the language of cataloging, the transcribing agency, and the modifying agency. This field is logically connected with byte 39 of field 008, the cataloging source code. The appropriate NUC symbols are included in the following subfield codes.

$a—original cataloging agency

$b—language of cataloging (use List of Languages and Language Codes, published as Appendix II.C of *MARC Formats for Bibliographic Data*)

$c—transcribing agency

$d—modifying agency

Only subfield $d is repeatable. The Library of Congress will follow the policy of not including field 040 when field 008, byte 39, contains a blank, since this indicates the Library of Congress. Records supplied through the NACO Project at the library have code d in byte 39 of field 008 and will carry the appropriate NUC symbol of the institution that contributed the name heading in field 040, subfield $a. The symbol for the Library of Congress will be carried in subfield $c.[31]

Authentication Center (042)

This field anticipates the establishment of a national authority data base. It is presently envisioned that several authentication centers will review, and upgrade when necessary, authority records submitted by network participants. No codes are assigned for this field yet, but they will "be compatible with those assigned for other cooperative input projects."[32]

Geographic Area Code (043)

If there is a geographic area associated with the heading, this field contains the code for the area. This seven-character code consists of a combination of alphabetic characters and hyphens and is theoretically designed to provide a hierarchical breakdown between geographical and political entities. The list of possible codes is published as Appendix II.B of *MARC Formats for Bibliographic Data*. Field 052 can record a greater level of detail on geographic areas.[33]

Chronological Code or Date/Time (045)

This field provides yet another means of recording a distinctive feature about the heading in the authority record. It records date(s) and/or time(s) associated with the heading.[34] The authority format includes a detailed explanation of the construction of such codes that will not be repeated here.

Library of Congress Call Number (Series) (050)

This field contains the LC call number of those series that the Library of Congress has classified, as a whole or in part, as a collected set. It is used only for call numbers assigned by the Library. The field is repeatable so that different call numbers may be recorded for different ranges and dates.[35]

Geographic Classification Code (052)

This field is related to the 043 field, but it is more specific than the 043 geographic area code. The 052 code is derived from LC classification schedule G and it is formed simply by dropping the G from the classification schedule. There are two subfield codes, $a and $b. Subfield $a contains the geographic area code described above; the $b subfield contains the subarea code, which consists of one alphabetic character and one or more numeric characters derived from the LC classification schedule or the expanded Cutter lists (e.g., for Halifax, Nova Scotia: ƀ ƀ $ a 3 4 2 4 $ ƀ H 2).[36]

LC Classification Number (053)

This field contains the LC classification associated with an authority heading. Although the format does not state so explicitly, this field is only used in conjunction with subject headings. It may contain one or more classification numbers or range of numbers. The three subfields $a, $b, and $c are used to record the various possibilities.[37]

Dewey Decimal Classification Number (083)

This field serves the same purpose as the 053 field, but it contains the Dewey classification number associated with the heading. This field has codes for the first indicator that specify whether the full edition or the abridged edition is being documented. Subfield $2 specifies the edition number from which the number came.[38]

Local Call Number (Series) (090)

This field is similar in purpose and structure to the 050 field. It contains any locally assigned call number *of a series* if all or part of the series is classified as a set. The codes are as follows:

a—classification number

b—item number

c—volumes/dates to which call number applies[39]

Headings

The 1xx Fields

These are the only heading fields that are analogous to the bibliographic record fields of the same type. There are six of them:

100—personal name

110—corporate name

111—conference or meeting name

130—uniform title

150—topical subject

151—geographic name

Like all variable fields, each of these can have assigned values for both indicators. In the 100 field, for example, the first indicator specifies the type of personal name—forename only, single surname, multiple surname, or name of family. The 110 field has three possible values for the first indicator—surname (inverted), geographic name with corporate or form subheading, and/or title and name in direct order. The second indicator of all 1xx fields is used to specify the number of nonfiling characters. Each of these fields contains several subfields, the designation of which is particular to the field in question. The subfields allow for adequate data definition and include all elements prescribed by AACR2, as well as by earlier versions of the rules.[40]

Established Name Heading (100)

This field contains a personal name heading established in accordance with currently accepted rules of cataloging. Numerous subfields cover all types of qualifiers and other information required for personal name headings. Of particular interest to those establishing names under the guidance of AACR2, the $q subfield is used to define the fuller form qualification of a name, as in

Tolkien, J. R. R. $q (John Ronald Revel), $d 1828-1901

The field may also include form headings for personal names, as in

Jesus Christ $k in fiction, drama, poetry, etc.

where $k is the form subheading.

Furthermore, this field is also used to transmit name/title headings, such as

Dostoyevsky, Fyodor, $d 1821-1881. $t Prestuplenie i nakazanie.

where $d defines birth and/or death dates and $t is the title of a work.

Since the list of subfields and their application is detailed and not central to the discussion here, the reader may refer to the MARC authority format itself.[41]

Established Corporate Name Heading (110)

There is much confusion over the use of this field in relation to the 111 field and the 151 field. First let us discuss the differences between the 110 field and the 151 field. Most corporate name headings are readily identifiable and not easily confused with the names of geographic entities. No one would mistake Arthur D. Little, Inc., for an island in the Caribbean. However, the question whether to place the name of a political jurisdiction, which is a corporate body (e.g., Albania), in the 110 field or the 151 field is one that may keep many people busy for many years to come. The guidelines following the tag number in the authority format state, "Geographic names followed by a corporate or form subheading and/or a title are considered corporate names (tags x10); geographic names alone or followed by subject subdivisions are considered geographic names (tags x51)."[42] If these guidelines are followed, there should be no problem in assigning a particular name to its proper tag. The reasons for the curious split between geographic names and political jurisdictions and the conceptual and processing problems it causes were discussed in Chapter 2.

The first indicator serves to specify what type of name occurs after the tag. The codes for the indicator are:

0—surname (inverted)

1—geographic name with corporate or form subheading and/or title

2—name (direct order)[43]

There is also frequent confusion in processing about where to put names of meetings or conferences whose first element is a corporate body in the usual sense—for example:

Kommunisticheskaia partiia Sovetskogo Soiuza. S"ezd

(Communist Party of the Soviet Union. Congress)

Some argue that since the entire heading is the name of a meeting, it belongs unequivocally in field 111. Others maintain that since the first element of the conference/meeting name is a corporate body in the usual sense, it unequivocally belongs in field 110. The authority format has not commented on this situation, but by force of example it seems that the preference is to place such headings in field 110 and treat the name of the conference as a subordinate body. The example given in the authority format bears this out:

> 110   20$aLabor   Party   (Great   Britain).$bConference$n(72nd   :$d1972
> :$cBlackpool, Lancashire)[44]

Some bibliographic utilities state this preference explicitly and give further examples and guidance in their system manuals for authority work/authority file use.[45]

Like the 100 field, the 110 field has many subfields that can accommodate all the distinct parts of a corporate name. There is no special subfield code, however, for a qualifier of a corporate name. So the heading

> Vsesoiuznyi institut nauchnoi i tekhnicheskoi informatsii (Soviet Union)

would appear as

> 110   20$aVsesoiuznyi   institut   nauchnoi   i   tekhnicheskoi   informatsii
> (Soviet Union)

The name and the qualifier all appear in subfield $a.

Established Conference or Meeting Name (111)

Confusion about the use of this field and field 110 is discussed in the immediately preceding section, Established Corporate Name Heading.

Established Uniform Title (130)

Problems with the processing of uniform titles, especially when such titles are part of a specific author's *oeuvre,* have been discussed in Chapter 2. For convenience, the definition of the term *uniform title* is repeated here:

> A uniform, or standardized, title heading is intended to bring together the records for various issues of a work which have been published under different titles and *which have not been entered under a personal or corporate name.* Uniform titles may include the names of radio and television programs, motion pictures, anonymous works, composite manuscripts or manuscript groups, some treaties and intergovernmental agreements, serials, and other works entered under title.[46] (Emphasis added.)

Again, that part of the definition stating that such titles have not been entered under a personal or corporate name is dependent on the cataloging rules in force at the time. For uniform titles entered under a personal or corporate name, the title is placed in the $t subfield of the 100, 110, or 111 field, as appropriate. OCLC now has 130 searchable fields, but the status of uniform titles placed in $t subfields of 100, 110, or 111 fields is still not clear. It is a problem for any type of cataloging but becomes especially burdensome in music cataloging, where almost every piece cataloged requires at least one uniform title.

As in the 110 field, if a corporate body is qualified, there is no subfield to define this type of data other than the $a subfield. So, for example, the heading

Voice of America

would appear in a machine-readable authority record as

130 0$aVoice of America (Radio program).

That is, there would be no subfield for the qualifier (Radio program).

Topical Subject (150)

In records distributed by the Library of Congress, this field will contain a topical subject heading authorized for use. The subject heading system used for the formation of the topical subject heading is identified in the 008 field, byte 11. This byte in the 008 field has the following possible codes:

a—Library of Congress

b—LC Children's Literature

c—National Library of Medicine

d—National Agricultural Library

k—National Library of Canada English Headings

v—National Library of Canada French Headings

z—other

n—not applicable (not a subject heading)[47]

Established Geographic Name Heading (151)

The authority format identifies the following as geographic names: "natural features, geographic regions, archaeological sites, parks, and political jurisdictions, alone or followed by *subject* subdivision."[48] On the other hand, "geographic names with a *corporate or form subheading and/or a title* are considered corporate names."[49] (Emphases added.)

References and Tracings

Since the authorized form of name was chosen according to current catalog-ing rules and therefore likely required not only a choice between different forms of the name, but also a decision to append or omit certain other information (such as titles and birth and death dates), any intelligent user might well search for the name in question under a discarded alternative. In order to accommodate such behavior, catalogers, or those who prepare authority records, provide the means to retrieve the authorized form of name through its variants. Variant forms are generically referred to as cross-references. They include not only variants that may be different because of their fullness (Wessells, M. B. vs. Wessells, Michael Bernard) or variants that are the result of chosen pseudonyms (Lenin, Vladimir Ilich vs. Ulîanov, Vladimir Ilich), but also two or more names both of which are or were valid (Institute of Scientific and Technical Information vs. National Institute of Scientific and Technical Information).

Cross-references can be of two types—*see from* references and *see also from* references. The first and second examples above are *see from* references—one name has been chosen as an authorized form and the other form or forms are unautho-rized variants. Through the mechanics of the authority file, the user is directed from the variant form to *see* the authorized form. For *see also from* references, the type shown in the third example, *both* forms are authorized forms of names, because they were both legitimate names of that institution at different periods of time. Hence, when a user retrieves one of these forms, thinking that this is the only form that exists, he or she is directed to *see also* the other authorized form. In such cases, each name will probably refer to a different class of bibliographic records.

A further distinction is made for such variant names and subjects, the distinc-tion between references and tracings. In its most basic form the difference between a reference and a tracing consists of the inclusion or omission of the imperatives *see from* and *see also from*. A tracing omits such imperatives; a reference includes them (or occasionally other additional information). So, referring again to example one, let us assume that we have chosen the form

Wessells, M. B.

as our authorized form. One tracing for this name would be

Wessells, Michael Bernard

The reference for this record would be

Wessells, Michael Bernard
    see
Wessells, M. B.

It would include the imperative *see from* as well as the authorized form referred to. For the third example, on the other hand, the authorized heading

Institute of Scientific and Technical Information

would include the imperative *see also from* along with the other, newer name for the institute. The reference would look like this:

Institute of Scientific and Technical Information

    see also

National Institute of Scientific and Technical Information

It might also include the information that the name change occurred in 1955.

With this background in mind, the following explanation from *Authorities: A MARC Format* will be clear.

> In most instances, a reference to a heading is not carried explicitly in the machine-readable authority record. Instead, a tracing for the reference is carried in a 4xx or 5xx field in the authority record for the established heading to which the reference refers. A 4xx field is used for a "see from" tracing containing a variant form of the established heading. A 5xx is used for a "see also from" tracing containing a related established heading. The actual reference can be displayed from a tracing as desired, based on codes provided in the control subfield $w....
>
> When a meaningful (so-called "complex") reference cannot be constructed from one or more tracings by a display program, the actual text of the reference is carried either in a separate reference record or in a note field (including field 360) within the authority record. In either case, the 1xx field, containing the heading referred from, is combined for display with a field which contains the remaining text of the reference.[50]

Before a discussion of the authority record/"reference" record dichotomy, or the various note fields like the 360 field, a description of the 4xx and 5xx fields is in order.

The Tracing Fields 4xx and 5xx

As described above, these fields contain the tracings for *see from* (4xx) and *see also from* (5xx) references. The 4xx fields contain tracings for variant forms of the authorized form of name carried in the 1xx field. The types of 4xx fields follow the same pattern as the 1xx fields:

400—personal name tracing

410—corporate name tracing

411—conference name tracing

430—uniform title tracing

450—topical subject tracing

451—geographic name tracing

Like the 1xx counterparts, each of these fields contains a tag (4xx), two indicators, and subfields. The subfields allow the definition of additional information required by cataloging rules to form the name. In the interest of brevity, detailed explanations of each of these fields are omitted. The curious user is invited to refer to *Authorities: A MARC Format* itself. A few examples, however, may serve to show the relationship between the 1xx field and a 4xx field in the same record. The examples are taken from *Authorities: A MARC Format.*

400—personal name
    100 10$aBrowning, Elizabeth Barrett,$d1806-1861
    400 10$aBrauning, Elizaveta Barrett,$d1806-1861

Note the differences in spelling for the first name and surname.

410—corporate name
    110 20$aSchweizerisches Rotes Krauz
    410 20$aCroix-Rouge suisse

Note the different, nonofficial form of name.

411—conference name
    111 20$aSymposium on Endocrines and Nutrition$d(1956 :$cUniversity of Michigan)
    411 20$aNutrition Symposium$d(1956 :$cUniversity of Michigan)

Note the different name of the symposium.

430—uniform title
    130 0$aNibelungenlied
    430 0$aLied der Nibelungen

Note the different form of name for the epic.

450—*see from* tracing, topical subject
    150 0$aFederal aid to education
    450 0$aEducation$xFederal aid

451—*see from* tracing, geographic name
    151 0$aCentral Europe
    451 0$aEurope, Central

The 5xx fields follow the same pattern as the 1xx and 4xx fields:

500—personal name tracing

510—corporate name tracing

511—conference name tracing

530—uniform title tracing

550—topical subject tracing

551—geographic name tracing

Examples of these *see also from* tracings follow. The examples are taken from *Authorities: A MARC Format.*

500—personal name
    100 00$aPseudo-Brutus
    500 10$aBrutus, Marcus Junius,$d85?-42B.C.

510—corporate name
    110 20$aDunedin Savings Bank
    510 20waaOtago Savings Bank

511—conference name
    111 20$aMeeting in the Matter of Pollution of Lake Erie and Its Tributaries
    511 20waaaConference in the Matter of Pollution of Lake Erie and Its Tributaries

Note the other valid form of conference heading and subfield $w (to be discussed below).

530—uniform title
    130 0$aKoran$xReadings
    530 0wgaKoran$xCriticism, Textual

Note the different subheading.

550—topical subject
    150 0$aElectronic data processing$xData preparation
    550 0$aInput design, Computers

551—geographic name
    151 0$aKabwe (Zambia)
    551 0waaBrokes Hill (Zambia)

As mentioned earlier in the quotation about the generation of references from tracings, in some cases references cannot be generated from the tracings in the 4xx and 5xx fields. These are the so-called complex references. In turn these complex references may require either a note carried in the authority record itself or an entirely different reference record, very similar to an authority record except that the 1xx field does not carry an established form of heading.

The reference record is used when "the heading referred from is not an established form of heading."[51] The tracing for the unestablished form of heading is carried in the 1xx field. The note is used for complex references when the heading referred from is an established form of heading. Table A.5 (see p. 102) shows the different types of references made for both reference records and notes in authority records.

In order to understand the table and the elements in it, a description is necessary of fields 260 and 360, the control subfield $w, and the note fields (excluding for the time being the series treatment fields).

260 Field–General Explanatory See From *Reference (Subjects)*

This field is only used in a reference record for subjects in order to give the text for a general explanatory *see from* reference. As pointed out above, in subject reference records the 1xx field contains an established form of subject referred from. The 260 field would look like this:

    008 byte 9 b(reference record, untraced reference)
    150 0$aTravel regulations
    260 $isubdivision$aOfficials and employees—Travel regulations$iunder coun-
            tries, government departments, cities, etc.; and subdivision$aTravel
            regulations$iunder special categories of officials, e.g.,$aJudges—Travel
            regulations.

The unusual use of subfield $i is intended to differentiate the subject heading itself (established or unestablished) from the explanatory text.

360 Field–General Explanatory See Also From *Reference (Subjects)*

This field is used only in an authority record to provide a general explanatory *see also from* reference for subjects.

    008 byte 9 a(authority record)
    150 0$aCollectors and collecting
    360 $isubdivisions$aCollectors and collecting$iand$aCollection and preserva-
            tion$iunder names of objects collected, e.g.,$aPostage-stamps—Collec-
            tors and collecting; Zoological specimens—Collection and preservation.

Neither the 260 nor the 360 field is used for name authority records.

Table A.5.
Complex References

	see from (subjects)	see from (names)	see also from (subjects)	Information/ history reference (names)	Cataloger-generated see also from (names)	Cataloger-generated see from reference (names)
Reference Records	1xx field & 260 field These references are not traced in any authority record.	1xx field & 666 field				1xx & 664 fields Reference traced in authority record for name referred to Byte 3 of $w in 4xx is code b
Authority Records			360 field Reference not traced	665 field Reference traced in 5xx with byte 3 of $w as code d	663 field Reference traced in 5xx with byte 3 of $w as code c	

Control Subfield $w

In the preliminary edition of *Authorities: A MARC Format,* the control subfield $w was used *in each field* of an authority record and contained twenty-four bytes. Appendix II of the first edition of *Authorities: A MARC Format* contains specifications for converting a control subfield $w from the former twenty-four bytes to the revised maximum four bytes. The four bytes consist of a variable number of fixed-position, one-character alphabetic codes that specify two kinds of information about the tracing. The codes tell "whether a tracing is restricted to the reference structure of a particular type of authority" and "whether special instructions apply to the display of the tracing in the form of the reference."[52] The four fixed positions can also contain a code that gives more specific information pertaining to these two categories, but it is not mandatory that all four fixed positions carry meaningful codes. "If the restrictions/special instructions do not apply to a given field, the control subfield need not be used in that field. However, if the control subfield is used, the coding of any position mandates that each prior position be explicitly coded also. The fill character may be used in any position required solely because a subsequent position is coded."[53]

In a given system, these codes can be used to generate print constants if the authority system is paper based, or they may be used to generate displays that enable the naive user to understand the highly structured information provided in the naked format. The control subfield $w is only used for the 4xx and 5xx fields and is the first subfield in any individual field. The four positions defined for control subfield $w are shown in Table A.6.

Table A.6.
Outline of Control Subfield $w.

Data element	Number of characters	Character position
Special relationship code	1	0
Tracing use restriction code	1	1
Earlier cataloging rules code	1	2
Reference display/print restriction code	1	3

The special relationship code specifies the relationship between a tracing and an authorized heading. Relationships that may be specified are earlier heading, later heading, acronym, musical composition (not valid under AACR2), broader term, narrower term (for subjects), reference instruction phrase in subfield $i, and not applicable.

The tracing use restriction code specifies the authority reference structure in which a given tracing is appropriate. Possibilities exist for name authority reference structure only, subject authority reference structure only, series authority reference structure only, and various combinations of these three basic types, such as subject and series, name and series, name and subject, etc.

The earlier cataloging rules code is used to specify whether a 4xx tracing is in the form of the heading authorized for use under earlier cataloging rules. The only values allowed for this are a code indicating that the form was established under earlier rules or the fill character (ƀ). The authority format, does, however, give this caveat: "Library of Congress practice: Until all tracings on name authority records created prior to 1981 have been evaluated and the authority records updated, some 4xx fields will be coded with earlier values b (AACR1), c (AACR2), or d (non-AACR form used with AACR2)."[5 4]

Finally, the reference display/print restriction code indicates whether a reference is to be displayed from a 4xx or 5xx tracing. The code values specify whether no reference is to be made at all or whether no reference is to be made because it is generated elsewhere, such as in a separate reference record or in a 665 field (history note).

Notes (Excluding Series Treatment Notes)

The following note fields have been defined in the first edition of the authority format:

663—cataloger-generated *see also from* reference (names)

664—cataloger-generated *see from* references (names)

665—information or history reference (names)

666—general explanatory reference (names)

667—usage or scope (names)

668—characters in nonroman alphabets

670—source data found

675—source data not found

678—epitome

680—scope note (subjects)

681—example under/note under (subjects)

682—deleted heading information

Some of these note fields are used only with name authority records, some only with subject authority records, and some only with reference records. In addition, some require or go hand-in-hand (or byte-by-byte) with other coding in the record, such as the 663, 664, and 665 fields and subfield $w, and field 682, used only when byte 5 of the leader is coded x. Table A.7 (p. 106) shows at a glance what types of records the individual fields are used for and other requirements in the way of leader information.

Table A.7.
Note Fields and Their Uses in the Authority Format.

Note Field	Names	Subjects	Authority Rec.	Reference Rec.	Other
663	✓		✓		c in byte 3, $w, 5xx
664	✓			✓	b in byte 3, $w, 4xx
665	✓		✓		d in byte 3, $w, 5xx
666	✓			✓	
667	✓		✓		
668	✓		✓		
670	✓	✓	✓		
675	✓	✓	✓		
678	✓		✓		
680		✓	✓		
681		✓	✓		
682	✓	✓	✓	✓	x in byte 5 of leader

Even though each of the note fields has a specific name, it is often difficult, even for the experienced cataloger, to determine their exact use. The following definitions of each of the note fields are offered to help distinguish one note field from another and to serve as a ready reference at the terminal for users of authority records.

Cataloger-generated See Also From *Reference (Names) (663)*

This field is used when a required *see also from* reference for names cannot be constructed from the content of one or more 5xx fields. Therefore it is also known as a complex reference. Library of Congress practice dictates that from 1981 on, these   references are made "only when the relationship cannot be adequately covered by multiple simple references produced from tracing fields."[5 5] An example of field 663 follows.

Authority record 1:

    ØØ8 byte 9 = a (authority record)
    [1ØØ]   1Ø$aØrn, B.
    [5ØØ]   1Ø$wnnnc$aBader, Mette
    [5ØØ]   1Ø$wnnnc$aChristensen, Hans Jørn
    [5ØØ]   1Ø$wnnnc$aDøør, Jørgen, 1933-
    [663]   ƀƀaJoint pseudonym of Mette Bader, Hans Jørn Christensen,
        Jørgen Døør and others; see also$bBader, Mette$bChristensen,
        Hans Jørn$bDøør, Jørgen, 1933-

Authority record 2:

    ØØ8 byte 9 = a (authority record)
    [1ØØ]   1Ø$aBader, Mette
    [5ØØ]   1Ø$wnnnc$aØrn, B.
    [663]   ƀƀ$aFor works of this author written in collaboration with
        Hans Jørn Christensen, Jørgen Døør and others, see
        also$bØrn, B.

Authority record 3:

    ØØ8 byte 9 = a (authority record)
    [1ØØ]   1ØaChristensen, Hans Jørn
    [5ØØ]   1Ø$wnnnc$aØrn, B.
    [663]   ƀƀ$aFor works of this author written in collaboration with
        Mette Bader, Jørgen Døør and others, see also$bØrn, B.

Authority record 4:

    ØØ8 byte 9 = a (authority record)
    [1ØØ]   1ØaDøør, Jørgen,$d1933-
    [5ØØ]   1Ø$wnnnc$aØrn, B.
    [663]   ƀƀ$aFor works of this author written in collaboration with
        Mette Bader, Hans Jørn Christensen and others, see
        also$bØrn, B.

Cataloger-generated **See From** *Reference (Names) (664)*

Like the 663 field, this is used when a required *see from* reference for names cannot be constructed solely from the content of one or more 4xx fields. An example of field 664 follows.

Reference record:

    008 byte 9 = c (reference record--traced reference)
    [100] 10$aFischer, S.
    [664] ƀƀ$asee$bFisher, S.$bFisher, Shmuel, 1917-

Authority record 1:

    008 byte 9 = a (authority record)
    [100] 10$aFisher, S.
    [400] 10$wnnnb$aFischer, S.

Authority record 2:

    008 byte 9 = a (authority record)
    [100] 10$aFisher, Shmuel, 1917-
    [400] 10$wnnnb$aFischer, S.

Information or History Reference (Names) (665)

This field is used to provide historical information about the heading. As of 1981, generation of new history references was discontinued by the Library of Congress.[56]

General Explanatory Reference (Names) (666)

This field is only used in reference records to provide information to assist in searching or filing. An example of the field follows.

    008, byte 9 = b (reference record--untraced reference)
    [100] 00$aDe la
    [666] ƀƀ$aFor names beginning with a prefix, search under the
           prefix (under each element if the prefix is made up of multiple
           words) as well as under the name following the prefix.

Usage or Scope (Names) (667)

This field contains usage or scope information about established headings, such as "not to be confused with Smith, Archibald."

Characters in Nonroman Alphabets (668)

Characters in nonroman alphabets that represent the heading are carried in this field.

Source Data Found (670)

This field contains a citation to a reference source for information about the heading established. This is the one field LC catalogers are required to use to document the evidence used to determine the form of name chosen for the heading. The conventional order for recording data in this field is main entry of work, title (if different from main entry), edition, date of publication: place in publication where form of name found (transcription), other place (transcription).[57] Under the Total On-line System for Cataloging Activities (TOSCA), the Library of Congress restricts the searching to the existing LC machine-readable records. If a heading is found on a MARC record that was cataloged *and* input by the library, this data is also recorded. A source data found note could look like this:

> Zhemchuzhiny Zhigulei, 1982: verso t.p. (Stepan Kuzmenko) colophon (Stepan Egorovich Kuzmenko)
>
> LC in OCLC, 11-5-84 (Hdg.: Kuz'menko, Stepan Egorovich)

Source Data Not Found (675)

This field contains citations to sources where no information about the heading was found.

Epitome (678)

This field is used to record biographical, historical, or other information about the heading. This field could also contain data that appears elsewhere in the record.

Scope Note (Subjects) (680)

This field indicates the use of a subject heading and describes the difference between overlapping or similar headings.

Example Under/Note Under (Subjects) (681)

This field serves as a tracing for another record in which the heading appears as an example in a general explanatory *see from* or *see also from* reference (fields 260 and 360) or in a scope note (field 680).

Deleted Heading Information (682)

When a record is deleted, a deleted record is issued with value x in leader byte 5 (record status). This note explains why the record was deleted.

Series Treatment Fields

The final type of field is the series treatment field. These fields were not mentioned at all in the preliminary edition of the authority format. They were designed to aid in the transfer of series treatment information among different institutions, since the bibliographic communications formats do not provide such information. These fields tend to be more complicated than most, primarily because of the inherent complexity of series and serials themselves. When using and referring to the series treatment fields, it is important to keep in mind that they record information about the *treatment* of series in different institutions. This *treatment* is based on manifest facts about the series itself, such as beginning and ending dates, numbering peculiarities, and place and publisher/issuing body, as well as the way the series was treated in various institutions regarding analysis practice, tracing practice, and classification practice.

In cases in which an institution has treated a series as a serial, certain series treatment fields, such as 640 (dates of publication and volume designation), 641 (numbering peculiarities), and 643 (place and publisher/issuing body) will conform to fields in the bibliographic record and repeat the information contained there. Usually missing from the bibliographic record, however—primarily because there is no designated field for such information—is whether the library that cataloged the series as a serial decided to analyze the serial (if it in fact permitted analysis), or how the volumes of the serial are classified (as a collection or separately). In cases in which the series was treated as a series and used as part of the bibliographic information of the bibliographic record, it is necessary to determine whether such a series was traced or simply given in a note. The series treatment fields in the authority record provide such information. There are seven such fields:

640—dates of publication and volume designation

641—numbering peculiarities

642—series numbering example

643—place and publisher/issuing body

644—analysis practice

645—tracing practice

646—classification practice

A brief description of each field follows.

Dates of Publication and Volume Designation (640)

This field contains the beginning and/or ending dates of publication and/or the volume designation of a series. It is similar to the information contained in field 362 of the bibliographic record (serials format) but lacks the cataloging code restrictions placed on that information. Field 640 should be kept separate from field 642, which gives an example of the form of series numbering designation to be used in series-added entries.

Numbering Peculiarities (641)

This field contains the same information as field 515 of the serials format. It is used to record notes that cite peculiarities or irregularities in numbering.

Series Numbering Example (642)

This field contains an example of the numbering scheme and form to be used in subfield $v of the series-added entry fields of the bibliographic formats.

Place and Publisher/Issuing Body (643)

As the title implies, this field records the place of publication and the name of the publisher/issuing body.

Analysis Practice (644)

This field contains a code to show whether all the volumes of a series are analyzed, only some of them analyzed, or none of them analyzed.

Tracing Practice (645)

This field contains a code to show whether the series is used in bibliographic records as a series-added entry tracing or as an untraced series note. It also includes the volumes/dates and the institution/copy to which this practice applies.

Classification Practice (646)

Like its related fields, 644 and 645, this practice indication field contains a one-character code to indicate whether the volumes of a series are cataloged as a collection, with the main series, or separately.

NOTES

1.   *The MARC Pilot Project: Final Report on a Project Sponsored by the Council on Library Resources, Inc.*, prepared by Henriette D. Avram (Washington, D.C.: Library of Congress, 1968), 1.

2.   Lucia J. Rather, "Exchange of Bibliographic Information in Machine-readable Form," *Library Trends* 25:3 (January 1977), 625-644, esp. 631-636; *The US MARC Formats: Underlying Principles, Library of Congress Information Bulletin* 42:19 (May 9, 1983), 148-152.

3.   Rather, "Exchange of Bibliographic Information," 634-635.

4.   John C. Attig, "The Concept of a MARC Format," *Information Technology and Libraries* 1:1 (March 1982), 15.

5. Ibid.

6. Ibid.

7. *Authorities: A MARC Format: Specifications for Magnetic Tapes Containing Authority Records,* preliminary ed. (Washington, D.C.: Library of Congress, 1976), 3.

8. *Authorities: A MARC Format,* 1st ed. (Washington, D.C.: Library of Congress, Processing Services, 1981), 2.

9. Ibid., 8.

10. Ibid., 9.

11. Ibid., 14.

12. Ibid.

13. Ibid., 12.

14. Ibid., 6.

15. Ibid., 20.

16. Ibid., 23.

17. Edwin Buchinski, "Authorities: A Look into the Future," in *What's in a Name: Control of Catalogue Records through Automated Authority Files,* ed. and comp. Natsuko Y. Furuya (Toronto: University of Toronto Press, 1978), 203-224; Michael Gorman and Robert H. Burger, "Serial Control in a Developed Machine System," *Serials Librarian* 5(1):13-26 (Spring 1982).

18. *Authorities: A MARC Format,* 1st ed., 24.

19. Ibid., 27.

20. Ibid., 28.

21. Ibid., 29.

22. Ibid., 30.

23. Ibid., 32.

24. Robert H. Burger, "Data Definition and the Decline of Cataloging Quality," *Library Journal* 108(8):1924-1926 (October 15, 1983).

25. *Authorities: A MARC Format,* 1st ed., 33, note 1.

26. Ibid., 34.

27. Ibid., 35.

28. Ibid., 36.

29. Ibid., 37.

30. Ibid., 38.

31.   Ibid., 39.

32.   Ibid., 40.

33.   Ibid., 41.

34.   Ibid., 42.

35.   Ibid., 45.

36.   Ibid., 46.

37.   Ibid., 47.

38.   Ibid., 48.

39.   Ibid., 49.

40.   See below under "Established Conference or Meeting Name" (field 111), p. 95.

41.   *Authorities: A MARC Format,* 1st ed., 50-51.

42.   Ibid., 52.

43.   Ibid.

44.   Ibid., 53.

45.   Australian Bibliographic Network, *Authority Control Manual,* 29. National Library of Australia, Version:11Aug1981.

46.   *Authorities: A MARC Format,* 1st ed., 56.

47.   Ibid., 58, 23.

48.   Ibid., 59.

49.   Ibid.

50.   Ibid., 60.

51.   Ibid.

52.   Ibid., 62.

53.   Ibid.

54.   Ibid., 66.

55.   Ibid., 103.

56.   Ibid., 107.

57.   Library of Congress, "Descriptive Cataloging Manual," Chapter Z1, 27.

SELECTED BIBLIOGRAPHY

Auld, Larry. "Authority Control: An Eighty-Year Review." *Library Resources and Technical Services* 26:319-330 (October/December 1982).

Avram, Henriette D. "Authority Control and Its Place." *Journal of Academic Librarianship* 9(6):331-335.

Buchinski, Edwin J., William L. Newman, and Mary Joan Dunn. "The Automated Authority Subsystem at the National Library of Canada." *Journal of Library Automation* 9(4):279-298 (December 1976).

————. *Initial Considerations for a Nationwide Data Base.* Network Planning Paper 3. ed. Henriette D. Avram and Sally McCallum. Washington, D.C.: Library of Congress, 1978.

————. "The National Library of Canada Authority Subsystem: Implications." *Journal of Library Automation* 10(1):28-40 (March 1977).

Burger, Robert H. "Artificial Intelligence and Authority Control." *Library Resources and Technical Services* 28(4):337-345 (October/December 1984).

————. "Data Definition and the Decline of Cataloging Quality." *Library Journal* 108(18):1924-1926 (October 15, 1983).

————. "Retrospective Conversion of Catalog Records to Machine-Readable Form: Past Attempts, Continuing Problems and Future Prospects." *Cataloging and Classification Quarterly* 3(1):27-40 (Fall 1982).

Clement, Hope E. A. "An International MARC Network." *International Cataloguing*, October/December 1981, 44-46.

Council on Library Resources, Inc., Bibliographic Service Development Program. "An Integrated Consistent Authority File Service for Nationwide Use." *Library of Congress Information Bulletin* 39:244-248 (July 11, 1980).

Council on Library Resources, Inc., Bibliographic Service Development Program, Task Force on a Name Authority File Service. *The Name Authority Cooperative/Name Authority File Service.* Washington, D.C.: Council on Library Resources, Inc., May 1984.

Cutter, Charles A. *Rules for a Dictionary Catalog,* 4th ed., rewritten. U.S. Bureau of Education, Special Report on Public Libraries, Pt. II. Washington, D.C.: Government Printing Office, 1904.

Dailey, Kazuko M., Grazia Jaroff, and Diana Gran. "RLIN and OCLC—Side by Side: Two Comparison Studies." *Advances in Library Administration and Organization* 1:69-125(1982).

Davison, Wayne E. "The WLN/RLG/LC Linked Systems Project." *Information Technology and Libraries* 2:34-36 (March 1983).

De Gennaro, Richard. "Library Automation and Networking Perspectives on Three Decades." *Library Journal* 108(7):629-635 (April 1, 1983).

Delsey, Tom. "IFLA Working Group on an International Authority System: A Progress Report." *International Cataloguing,* February/March, 1980, 10-12.

Farmer, Linda. *UNICAT/TELECAT: Alternatives to Full Authority Implementation: A Discussion Paper Prepared for the Management Committee's Working Group on Authorities.* Toronto: Council of Ontario Universities, Office of Library Coordination, 1979.

Fellows, Dorcas. *Cataloging Rules with Explanations and Illustrations.* 2nd ed., rev. and enlarged. New York: H. W. Wilson, 1922.

Freeman, Mitch. "A Conversation with Frederick G. Kilgour." *Technicalities* 1(7):5 (June 1981).

Furuya, Natsuko, ed. and comp. *What's in a Name: Control of Catalogue Records through Automated Authority Files.* Edwin J. Buchinski, "Authorities: A Look into the Future," pp. 203-224; Jo Calk, "On-Line Authority Control in the Washington Library Network," pp. 135-160; Michael Gorman, "Authority Files in a Developed Machine System (With Particular Reference to AACR II)," pp. 179-202. Toronto: University of Toronto Press, 1978.

Ghikas, Mary W., ed. *Authority Control: The Key to Tomorrow's Catalog: Proceedings of the 1979 Library and Information Technology Association Institutes.* Ritvars Bregzis, "The Syndetic Structure of the Catalog," pp. 19-35; Barrie A. F. Burns, "Authority Control in Two Languages," pp. 128-157; Gwen Miles Culp, "Authority Control within the Washington Library Network Computer System," pp. 62-84; Michael Gorman, "Authority Control in the Prospective Catalog," pp. 166-180; Sally McCallum, "Evolution of Authority Control for a National Network," pp. 53-61; Mary A. Madden, "Is This Somehow Connected? The Vendor Perspective," pp. 85-96; R. Bruce Miller, "Authority Control in the Network Environment," pp. 36-52; Lucia J. Rather, "Authority Systems at the Library of Congress," pp. 158-165; Richard B. Sharpe, "An Author Name Authority File System," pp. 119-127; Michael B. Wessells and Robert Niehoff, "Synonym Switching and Authority Control," pp. 97-118. Phoenix, Ariz.: Oryx Press, 1982.

Gorman, Michael. "Anglo-American Cataloguing Rules, Second Edition." *Library Resources and Technical Services* 22(3):209-226.

Gorman, Michael, and Robert H. Burger. "Serial Control in a Developed Machine System." *Serials Librarian* 5(1):13-26 (Spring 1982).

Gorman, Michael, and Paul Winkler, eds. *Anglo-American Cataloguing Rules,* 2nd ed. Chicago: ALA, 1978.

Henderson, Kathryn Luther. "Great Expectations: The Authority Control Connection." *Illinois Libraries* 65(5):334-336.

Hildreth, Charles. *Online Public Access Catalogs: The User Interface.* Dublin, Ohio: OCLC, 1982.

Hill, Janet Swan. "The Authorities Institutes: Genesis and Design." *Illinois Libraries* 65(5):329-331.

_____. "The Northwestern Africana Project: An Experiment in Decentralized Bibliographic and Authority Control." *College and Research Libraries* 42:326-332 (July 1981).

Hillman, Diane. "Authority Control or the Key to Survival in the Eighties." *Law Library Journal* 73(4):929-957 (Fall 1980).

Hillman, Diane, and Christopher Sugnet. "Comparison of OCLC and RLIN: A Question of Quality." *Cataloging and Classification Quarterly* 4(1):65-72 (Fall 1983).

International Conference on Cataloging Principles, Paris, 1961. *Report.* London: International Federation of Library Associations, 1963.

King, Donald, and Edward C. Bryant. *Evaluation of Information Services and Products.* Arlington, Va.: Information Resources Press, 1971.

Lancaster, F. Wilfrid. "Evaluation within the Environment of an Operating Information Service." In *Information Retrieval Experiment,* ed. Karen Sparck Jones. London: Butterworths, 1981.

_____. *Guidelines for the Evaluation of Information Systems and Services.* Prepared for UNESCO under contract. N. p.: Unesco, 1978.

Larson, Ray R., and Vicki Graham. "Monitoring and Evaluating MELVYL." *Information Technology and Libraries* 2:93-104 (March 1983).

Library of Congress, Automated Systems Office. *MUMS Reference Guide.* Washington, D.C.: Library of Congress, March 1983.

_____. *National Level Authority Record,* preliminary ed. prep. Phyllis A. Bruns. Washington, D.C.: Library of Congress, 1982.

Library of Congress, Descriptive Cataloging Division. "Descriptive Cataloging Manual." Chapters N, Z1, and Z2.

Library of Congress, MARC Development Office. *Authorities: A MARC Format: Specifications for Magnetic Tapes Containing Authority Records.* Preliminary ed. (with addenda). Washington, D.C.: Library of Congress, 1976.

Library of Congress, Processing Services. *Authorities: A MARC Format.* 1st ed. Washington, D.C.: Library of Congress, 1981.

Library Trends 30(1) (Summer 1981). Special issue on Bibliometrics, William G. Potter, ed.

Lowry, Glenn R. "Creating a Computer-Based LC Name Authority Control Module for an Online Public Access Catalog." In *Proceedings of the Fifth National Online Meeting New York, April 10-12, 1984,* comp. Martha Williams and Thomas H. Hogan. Medford, N.J.: Learned Information, 1984.

Ludy, Lorene E., and Susan J. Logan. "Integrating Authority Control in an Online Catalog." In American Society for Information Science, *Proceedings of the ASIS Annual Meeting,* ed. Anthony A. Petraca, Celianna I. Taylor, and Robert S. Kohn. Vol. 19, pp. 176-178. ASIS, 1982.

_____. "LC Name Authority Tapes Used by Ohio State University Libraries." *Information Technology and Libraries* 3(1):69-71 (March 1984).

McCallum, Sally. "Statistics on Headings in the MARC File." *Journal of Library Automation* 14(3):194-201 (September 1981).

MacIntosh, Helen. "SHARAF: The Canadian Shared Authority File Project." *Library Resources and Technical Services* 26(4):345-352 (October/December 1982).

McPherson, Dorothy. *Authority Control in the University of California Union Catalog.* Division of Library Automation Working Paper 9. Berkeley, Calif.: Division of Library Automation, Office of the Assistant Vice President, Library Plans and Policies, University of California, May 1979, rev. October 1980.

Malinconico, Michael. "Bibliographic Data Base Organization and Authority File Control." *Wilson Library Bulletin* 54:36-45 (September 1979).

_____. "The Library Catalog in a Computerized Environment." *Wilson Library Bulletin* 51:53-64 (September 1976).

Malinconico, Michael, and James A. Rizzolo. "The New York Public Library Automated Book Catalog Subsystem." *Journal of Library Automation* 6:1:3-36 (March 1973).

Matson, Susan. "Desiderata for a National Series Authority File." *Library Resources and Technical Services* 26(4):331-344 (October/December 1982).

Matthews, Joseph R., and Joan Frye Williams. "The Bibliographic Utilities, Progress and Problems." *Library Technology Reports* 18(6):609-653 (November/December 1982).

Miller, R. Bruce. *Name Authority Control for Card Catalogs in the General Libraries.* Austin: University of Texas at Austin, General Libraries, 1981.

Mosey, Jeanette Gail. *Name Authority Work in OCLC Libraries: A Survey of Practices and Expectations.* Ph.D. diss., University of Southern California, January 1980.

New York Public Library. *ONLICATS: System Reference Manual.* Distributed by New York Public Library, Library Information & On-Line Network Systems. No date.

OCLC, Inc. *Name Authority: User Manual.* 2nd ed. Dublin, Ohio: OCLC, 1983.

Perreault, Jean M. "Authority Control, Old and New." *Libri* 32(2):124-148.

Potter, William G. "Lotka's Law Revisited." *Library Trends* 30(1):21-39 (Summer 1981).

_____. "When Names Collide: Conflict in the Catalog and AACR2." *Library Resources and Technical Services* 24:3-16 (Winter 1980).

Radke, Barbara S., Katharina E. Klemperer, and Michael G. Berger. "The User-Friendly Catalog: Patron Access to MELVYL." *Information Technology and Libraries* 1:358-371 (December 1982).

Research Libraries Group, Inc. *RLIN: System Reference Manual.* 1st ed. Stanford, Calif.: RLG, Inc., March 1984.

Runkle, Martin. "Authority in On-Line Catalogs." *Illinois Libraries* 62:603-606 (September 1980).

Salmon, Stephen R. "Characteristics of On-Line Public Catalogs." *Library Resources and Technical Services* 27:36-67 (January/March 1983).

Schmierer, Helen F. "The Relationship of Authority Control to the Library Catalog." *Illinois Libraries* 62:599-603 (September 1980).

Smith, Linda C. "Machine Intelligence vs. Machine-Aided Intelligence in Information Retrieval: A Historical Perspective." In *Research and Development in Information Retrieval: Proceedings, Berlin, May 18-20, 1982,* Lecture Notes in Computer Science 146, ed. Gerard Salton and Hans-Jochen Schneider. Berlin and New York: Springer-Verlag, 1983.

"Survey of Authority Files and Authority Control Systems: Brief Progress Report." *International Cataloguing* 7(3):26 (July/September 1978).

Taylor, Arlene G. "Authority Files in Online Catalogs: An Investigation of Their Value." *Cataloging and Classification Quarterly* 4(3):1-17 (Fall 1983).

Wajenberg, Arnold S. "The Use of LC Authority Records in the On-Line Catalogue of the University of Illinois at Urbana-Champaign." *Illinois Libraries* 65(5):331-333.

Wajenberg, Arnold S., and Michael Gorman. "The OCLC Data Base Conversion: A User's Perspective." *Journal of Library Automation* 14(3):174-189 (September 1981).

Washington Library Network. *Authority Reference Manual* (2nd draft). Olympia, Wash.: Washington State Library, April 1979.

_____. *Authority Maintenance Manual for Applications of WLN Software* (draft). Olympia, Wash.: Washington State Library, December 1982.

Wells, A. J. "The International MARC Network: A Study for an International Bibliographic Data Network." The IFLA International Office for UBC Occasional Paper 3. London: IFLA International Office for UBC, 1977.

Williams, Martha, Stephen W. Barth, and Scott E. Preece. "Summary Statistics for Five Years of the MARC Data Base." *Journal of Library Automation* 12(4):314-337 (December 1979).

Woods, Richard. "The Washington Library Network Computer System." *Online Review* 3(3)297-330 (1979).

INDEX

AACR2
> and authority work, 6
> headings compatible with, 36

Access points, 12. *See also* Headings
> choice of, 12, 13
> consistency of, 4
> definition of, 4
> determination of form of, 4, 14
> form of, 12
> retrieval and, 4
> uniqueness of, 4
> universe of, 14

Accuracy
> of data, 40
> of formats, 40-41

Acquisitions personnel as users of authority file, 31-32

ADABAS, 51, 57, 58

Adaptable Database System. *See* ADABAS

Alphabets, nonroman, 108

American National Standards Institute. *See* ANSI

AMIGOS Bibliographic Council, 69

Analysis practice field, 111

Anglo-American Cataloguing Rules, 2d ed. *See* AACR2

ANSI, 73

Application and treatment instructions, 20

Attig, John, 74

Authentication center, 91

Authority Control
> achievement of, 1
> change in concept of, in developed machine system, 70
> definition of, 2, 10
> as essential component of on-line catalog, 1
> evaluation of, 38
> history of, 9-10
> in lieu of evaluation, 39
> international implications of, 70
> province of, 3
> relationship to authority work, 3
> trends in, 68-69

Authority data
> change, rate of, 45
> changes in, 34-37
> legality of, 39-40
> machine-readable, development of, 73
> preparation of, 39-41
> revision of, 39-40
> sources for, 21-23
> transcription of
>> onto cards, 23-25
>> into machine-readable form, 25-27
> types of, 14-20

Authority file, 9
> behavior of, 42-43
> in card-based systems, 28
> changes in, method of, 52, 64
> coordination with bibliographic file, 33
> creation of, 28-30
> diachronic information about, 44
> electronic connection with bibliographic file, 34
> growth of
>> factors affecting, 44
>> measurement of, 43-44
> independent of bibliographic file, 33
> maintenance of, 28
> manual editing of, 51, 64
> as model for constructing other headings, 31
> as part of bibliographic file, 33-34
> and policy, 28-30
> as precedent file, 31